THE GOOD
AROUND US

THE GOOD AROUND US

Living and Leading from a Place of Joy,
Even in the Joyless Moments

Gael-Sylvia Pullen

Sylvia Global Media Network/Ghail Media Group

Seal Beach, California

Published 2020
Printed in the United States of America
Print ISBN: 978-1-7333452-0-0
E-book ISBN: 978-1-7333452-1-7
Library of Congress Control Number: 2019912149
For information or permission, address: info@gaelsylviapullen.com

DEDICATION

To my best friends: the fisherman, my husband Mark Allyn Pullen, aka "Handsome"; and the hockey player, our amazing son and generously wise soul, Angelo Sorrell Pullen.

Handsome, your first gift to me was asking me to dance to Teddy Pendergrass at Dillon's when you had a selection of seven other girls better dressed for the occasion. When I felt alone, still recovering from drowning in a sea of hope and unclear possibilities, wondering what to do with my life after my plans had been derailed, you came along. The songs we danced to into the early morning hours reconfirmed the power of prayer and kindness. And one song in particular, "Spend the Night" by Teddy Pendergrass, started us on our way. We haven't stopped dancing since then. The mental picture of that night remains with me decades later.

Your second gift to me was a dinner you cooked with fish you actually caught. At that point in life, I had been on lots of fishing expeditions filled with great anticipation, often returning home with fresh catches handed over as gifts from others who sympathized with my efforts. You not only fish, you teach others to be fishers of men. You're strong, confident, talented, and so generous with all your gifts that others follow your example — feeling free to catch what they need and release the rest so that greater bounty can be made available to others.

Your third gift to me was a weekend at Lake Arrowhead at a writer's retreat. You believed I had a story to share and prayed I'd find my writer's voice. Thank you for never ceasing to believe and for being able to hear me even when I stopped speaking of the dream deferred.

Fourth and grandest of gifts, our precious son, Angelo, father to Brave and Hero. You remain forever present as a father, coach, Monopoly expert, and Papa to our son's beautiful daughters. I watched and learned as you modeled faith in Christ in his life on and off the ice.

Angelo, the life lessons I learned during your thirty plus years of playing hockey remain with me today: I am to skate hard when needed (but always keep my eye on the puck and aim for the goal), know when to take the penalty with dignity (even when it seems unfair) for the sake of the team, and leave the tension, the bumps, the checks, the fights on the ice when the game is over. I'm brave because of you and Dad. You are my heroes and have instilled courage in me. It took almost forty years, but I found my written voice and present this as a thank you for gifting us with our granddaughters Brave and Hero.

I love you dearly,
Your Babe, Ya Mama, Your Sasha.

To a friend who is as close as a blood sister, Arlene Michiko Yee.

If marriage causes two families to become one, then somewhere in the world, there must be a word to describe when two friends become family. Who would have ever guessed that my meeting Gary in a class at Pomona College and a year later meeting you, a stranger, while brushing our teeth the day after landing in a foreign country, would cause a lifelong friendship as close as blood family. You could see what others couldn't when I shared what seemed impossible. For your lovingkindness and support in more ways than most will ever know, I thank you. This page is a special dedication page to you, Gary, Garett, Sabrina, and Josh, because you hold a special place in my heart forever. I love you.

With joy and gratitude,
Gael-Sylvia Brown Pullen

Not all storms come to disrupt your life,
some come to clear a path.

—Unknown

CONTENTS

INTRODUCTION

Let me float an idea past you. What would happen if you chose to look, lead, and act from a place of joy rather than fear and despair? Living our lives and viewing our world from a place of fear and despair just fuels more fear and despair, eventually causing bitterness and anger, not to mention making our lives more difficult. Hoping against all hope, dreaming new dreams, and taking action toward those dreams is a hard road when we're walking through the living nightmares we all—as human beings—have experienced. But for those who don't want to stay down and out, not trying—again and again and again—to live our best lives by grasping the dreams we see, isn't an option. That's where living from joy comes in.

We often look at life from a perspective of loss, shortcomings, and a desire to be and have *more*. As children, we're frequently encouraged to stop thinking and behaving with child-like thoughts, to be realistic, to see life and the world for what it is—hard. I've never bought into that way of thinking, which has made me appear odd in some circles. Believing the world to be a hard, dog-eat-dog world can be a lonely place to be when there's so much good around us. I never anticipated having my belief challenged. Until it was.

The Great Recession. The magnitude of loss, both local and global, had never been experienced by most Americans under the age of seventy-five. Like so many people, my husband and I lost years of hard work as our dreams were hit hard, our expectations diminished—a total collapse of twenty-five plus years of hard work achieved in and grounded in faith. To top it off, as our financial world fell down around us, beloved friends and family passed on, my husband was hit with Valley Fever, and I contracted a virus that affected my heart, leaving me weakened and pretty much bedridden for fifteen months.

A native Californian, I grew up with earthquakes. The unpredictable shaking of the ground beneath us is normal in this area. It may not happen daily or annually, but if you live in this space long enough, let alone grow up here, you'll experience it. You'll also be at a loss for words when trying to explain why we stay. But we all live with earthquakes in one form or another. No matter where you live, I'm sure you've experienced, or will experience, metaphorical ground shaking. First a few tremors, then maybe a major earthquake that will rock your world. Although everything around you may fall and the shattering of glass and dreams may pierce your soul, after the tremors subside, you can stand again and look for the good around you—the details of what was spared, the little things that allow you to get up, deeply inhale, and pick up the broken pieces to redesign a new perspective and a new life. During that tough earthquake in my life, after much thought, I came to the conclusion that while my fear didn't prevent the loss all around me, my faith truly saved me from being lost. Sadness and worry didn't (and couldn't) revive my soul. Being intentional in seeking joy recalibrated my heart.

Since then, I've learned to lead and live from a place of joy, shifting my perspective to an entrepreneur and philanthropist, holding even tighter to the faith that has sustained me, a marriage of thirty-eight years, our family, and a daily routine filled with expressions of gratitude squeezing into the crevasses of every cell of my being. This joy and gratitude burst forth into the lives of more than fifteen thousand women and girls globally in fewer than five years, when I founded Girls Fly in 2011. Girls Fly is an organization dedicated to inspiring women and girls and reaffirming the value of their lives and their most sacred dreams. It's my life experiences on steroids jammed into various events in which we provide safe places for girls to believe in themselves and their dreams. We show girls paths to making their dreams a reality, connecting the dots associated with their dreams and other important aspects of their lives, such as financial literacy, social responsibility, STEM+Art, international understanding, and international experiences. Few in the organization knew I had a broken heart. I doubled down on putting all negative self-talk in check. Through song, images, and words of wisdom drawn from others, I found joy. And finally, my heart began a journey to healing.

As it is for many children living in or near beach communities, the beach was always, and as an adult, still is, my favorite place to be—sunny, fun-filled days spent looking for seashells, building sandcastles, and being buried in the warmth of the sand. Calling on these memories during the challenges of adulthood has often soothed me, causing me to periodically want to run back to the place that provided comfort and joy. I live at the beach now. I returned in the midst of turmoil to heal my heart, both physically (The virus I'd contracted, myocarditis. affected my already broken heart) and emotionally, and collapsed there for the next fifteen months. For the most part, I could see the beach through my window. A beach I couldn't walk on, sand I couldn't touch, water I couldn't swim in. I spent hours pondering life's oddities, and how they still seemed to fit into a perfectly timed plan. Living near the ocean also reaffirmed for me the power of faith, the power to visualize, and the importance of holding on to a steadfast belief in future possibilities.

Every day I watched the boats in the marina outside my window. For many years, my husband was on track to be a semi-pro bass fisherman, so it seems we've always owned boats, even in the least likely places: the driest of deserts and the harshest of Ohio winters. Now, living so close to the water, surrounded by boats of every size and model, I became intrigued by how quickly I learned to distinguish sounds once drowned out and overpowered by all the goings on in the multiple restaurants we'd owned. Constant chaos and noise overload: timers going off, doors swishing open and closed, phones ringing, people yelling, car horns blasting, and non-stop demands coming from every direction.

The marine crews worked in a much quieter atmosphere than what I'd experienced during my past two-plus decades in the restaurant business, yet they reminded me daily of how important it was to clear away the things that surreptitiously become attached to us and must be cleared away. Their attentiveness to every detail was a reminder of how I needed the time to recover, a time of fine-tuning what I wanted to keep and of replacing what I no longer needed. We all need time to recharge and reevaluate, to notice the details, whether we're making New Year's resolutions, setting goals, working with the "believe it and see" concepts that many of us have used successfully, or thinking that we can fully be "the captain of our own ships and the masters of our own fate."

I'd be lying if I said that during the darkest hours of my grief and loss, you would have found me without fear, "the horror of the shade," as William Ernest Haley refers to it in his poem "Invictus."

Yet during that time of facing frightening circumstances and my own fear head-on, I had sense enough not to go down with the ship. I learned to let go and trust that everything would be all right. Sometimes the letting go was more of a ripping away, such as the loss of income and temporary loss of health. Most often, though, it was a gentle release, my choosing to acknowledge with sincere gratitude that the time served in other places, with other people, with cherished memories, were for a purpose now fulfilled, even if I had no idea yet what that purpose was. I knew it would become clear with time.

Through it all, I kept choosing not to abandon my faith. The constant planting and replanting of that faith in earlier years grounded me with a deep knowing that the earth would stop shaking and the seas would calm again. So I looked for the parts of my life that were still working and made conscious choices to create new memories from where I was.

All my life, I've felt drawn to exploring the outdoors, but the ocean, in particular, has held my full attention from my days growing up by the beach. The ocean is an environment that's completely unstable and unpredictable. It shows us who we really are. No matter how we define ourselves on land, no matter what our jobs, where we live, who we know, what we've accomplished, or what car we drive, our job on the ocean is to experience the never-ending wonder of something greater than we are, to understand the weather, to know the vessel that's getting us where we want to go, to experience three worlds through one adventure—life experiences seen on the surface, the entirely different world in the depths of the waters beneath us, and the spiritual realm accessed by faith. Stepping or swimming into new experiences is an adventure filled with valuable lessons that can carry us through periods of great calm as well as times when we feel the isolation found in the driest of deserts. The ocean speaks to me of the healing power of the seen and the unseen. It reminds me to trust the movement of predictable and unexpected journeys within the constant uncertainty.

Life is like the ocean. It has both profound and subtle moments when it moves us, shapes us, supports us, and awakens us to new possibilities and new shores. Life moves, it inspires, and it gives us reason to sing through all the changes. In the day-to-day moments of our lives, the world is always shifting, without our noticing. The ocean renews our faith and symbolizes how awe-inspiring and magnificent life can be. As a symbol, it reminds us that the power of the sea requires a shift in perspective, and that giving way to that shift, respecting it, allows us to grow. As I let the waves of life propel me safely back to shore in each of the stories in this book, I feel humbled by the power of Father God and Mother Nature. The ocean also reminds us of the importance of letting go of boundaries that will allow us to feel close to other people, to free us from our own self-imposed restrictions, to help break through the walls of our own limiting beliefs. Nature makes me feel powerless, and that awareness, in itself, is empowering. Coming home and living by the water reminded me how truly joyful I can be with or without having much. I never believed that striving for riches was the end-all-be-all. In fact, I was known for asking questions among our friends of all income levels, "When is enough, enough?" Yet living close to the ocean teaches me to live and appreciate the simple abundances life offers us daily.

This book is filled with personal stories to inspire living and leading from a place of faith and joy, even within joyless moments. It contains global life lessons I learned as a leader in business who was engaged in community and committed to the bottom line of action and accountability to get solutions. While reading the twenty-one stories in this book, I ask that you remain open.

In these pages, I believe you'll see for yourself that when you try living from faith and joy instead of fear and anger, while you may not quite be walking on water, your life will change as your perspective shifts. You'll start leading and living from an internal place of peace and joy, attracting more gratitude and laughter than you would have ever thought possible, especially when life is pretty crazy, yet still cool.

This book is interactive. At the beginning of each chapter, you'll find a Song for the Day that captures the essence of that chapter. You can scan the QR code to open a video of the song being performed. Just open the camera app on your phone, hold your phone steady for two to three seconds facing the QR code, and then, depending on your phone, you'll either see the URL to click or the video will open automatically.

While each story in this book builds on the one before, they can also be read out of order, as each story calls to you. It's my hope and prayer that within my stories you'll see with fresh eyes how your own life story has value and that where you are right now is perhaps the craziest, coolest place you could be. I also hope and pray that you start using joy as your barometer, that you fine-tune your ears and turn up the volume on the childlike voice that never left but has kept wanting you to believe it has value and a place in your life and this world.

PART

I

IGNITING A SENSE OF
Wonder

Every day, we're provided with a gift of curiosity, surprise, and a desire to learn something new. This gift comes wrapped within the word *Wonder*. To wonder is to experience a feeling of surprise, admiration, awe, and amazement, a feeling triggered by something beautiful, unexpected, unfamiliar, or inexplicable. Wonder also means to doubt or desire to know more. Although we may question and doubt, we must remember that no matter where we are in the world, we can trust our intuition to spark our desires to see the good around us, thus freeing us to understand how the unexpected, the unfamiliar, or the inexplicable can ignite beauty and joy.

You Know My Name
TASHA COBBS

GO BEYOND DISNEYLAND— AMERICA

"I only hope that we don't lose sight of one thing—
That it was all started by a mouse."

WALT DISNEY

I grew up in Southern California during the civil rights move-ment and the Vietnam War era. I was in elementary school when the draft began for that war, and in high school when it ended and the world transitioned to recovery, while civil rights made only incremental steps. I'm a beneficiary of both attempts at peace. The casualties of lost battles continue to be worth remembering. My perspective was influenced by images on the national news, in *Life*, *Ebony*, and *Jet* magazines—the taped and printed chronicling of war and other peoples' pain, Twiggy, Black power, afros, and dashikis.

Robust conversations took place at breakfast and dinner, with my parents, my four siblings, and me seated around the dining room table, and then more intense conversations at my grand-mother's house during Saturday dinner, Sunday breakfast, and

11

lunch following church, with a few friends or fellow church members attending. Dr. Martin Luther King, Jr. spoke at our church, Friendship Baptist, in Pasadena. I looked at my father, holding my little sister up so she could see. The resemblance of the man everyone was making a lot of fuss over to my father was uncanny (all this excitement for a man who resembled my dad!). Dr. King's visit is forever etched in my mind and his words influence my actions to this day.

Those years sitting in the church pew will stay with me forever — staring at the light filtering through the stained-glass windows, changing with the seasons, shining through my favorite window, the dove coming down when Jesus was baptized. All of us dressed in our Sunday best, the women with dead fox stoles looped around their necks, shawls with heads and beady marble eyes staring straight at me. Scared to death, I would bury my nose in my grandmother's armpit when one of those women sat next to me, as I listened to sermons about the power of love and demonstrating that love through civil action. Those times spent in worship, in heated conversations around the dining room table, and glued to the TV to watch Walter Cronkite on the *CBS Evening News* shaped my formative years. That time of unrest, despair, and hope showed me the necessity of sensitivity and brought a deeper awareness of the power of prayer.

The prayer part had been instilled in me at a much younger age. Each night, wearing my baby doll pajamas, I'd clutch my Dalmatian puppy and kneel with my then four siblings for bedtime prayer. We began with "Now I lay me down to sleep, I pray the Lord my soul to keep" then concluding with "God bless all the people who are calling out to You. ..." We prayed for the families of those who were fighting in the war, that their boys would come home, for my mom and dad's co-worker going through a difficult time, and for people called "missionaries" in other parts of the world. We prayed for God's presence, provisions for others, and kindness. We prayed for those we knew, people in other parts of the world, and family members we'd yet to meet. We'd close by naming each member of our immediate family.

My first memorable personal experience with the power of prayer was when we prayed to the Lord to stop the rain so we could go to a magical place called Disneyland the next day. We woke as excited as though it were Christmas morning. Filled with enthusiastic childlike expectation, we opened the wide-slatted, putty-colored venetian blinds (the window covering that morphed into mini blinds) to sunshine. We heard the sweet chirping of birds and my parents saying, "Pray and say, 'Thank You, Lord.' You guys get dressed; we're going to Disneyland!" Then we dropped to our knees to praise God and thank Him for His faithfulness.

The power of this feeling, these types of spiritual moments, fused with the fight for civil rights and the conversations around the movement, both within the privacy of our home and within the community, all stressing the importance of civil engagement, framed my childhood. These spiritual and worldly influences that went beyond ourselves and our home, along with the love, laughter, and safety I grew up in, shaped who I am.

It was during those times of civil engagement that I was introduced to the Peace Corps, and I began to think more about people in a world beyond the one I knew. I never mentioned my dreams of going into the Peace Corps to anyone but my grandmother, whose words "Don't stop seeing and believing" breathed life into me. I was a shy child, so shy that while my grandmother and I were extremely close, and she saw me more clearly than my own mother, she would introduce my siblings and me out of our birth order: "This is my oldest grandson, Allen," she'd say, skip me, point to my middle sister, "Barbara," younger sister, "Joice," youngest brother, "Bill," and then come back and introduce me as, "Oh. and this one, that's Timid." My grandmother could create magical moments with her colorful storytelling that empowered the quiet, observant, shy child I was to see and hear beyond the obvious. I learned to listen to myself and others. Most certainly, I learned to listen to the voice of God.

Because of the personality type I was born with — quiet, introverted, sensitive, and observant—I was able to see and hear what others would miss, including the voice of God. I heard Him not in a Hollywood flamboyant way, but in a quiet way I regarded as sacred, personal, and real. When others would feel sad, I could speak words of comfort and encouragement without them having opened their mouth to speak of their need. I would also hear the voice of direction with such clarity that I would have us change course on projects, highways, and life decisions for no apparent reason, only to learn later that we would wind up in the right place at just the right time.

My grandmother recognized that I heard Him and said, "The Lord will use that gift in you. Don't be afraid." Her words, her love, her life of listening and responding had brought her from the cottonfields of segregated Arkansas to the laundry rooms of segregated California in the early 1940s. As I watched her quietly love those in need, I felt I was witnessing a sacred act, one shared between the two of us. I'm sure my siblings witnessed the same expressions of her love, but some things are never spoken of, just acted upon and left at that.

Every day I saw how the acts of kindness grew out of our home environment, relationships, and atmosphere of love, and how easy it was to extend these acts of kindness to others. Her loving acts of kindness showed in how she touched other people's lives, hugged people, took food to people who were sick or hungry. I have so many warm memories of being with my grandmother—standing at her side, getting my face covered in flour as she rolled out biscuits, imitating her way of tying her apron strings as she prepared to cook the food and set the table in the same manner for everyone who sat down to eat at her table, including the sporadic appearance of the only homeless man in northeast Pasadena, known by everyone as "Scatman," who'd stop by for a visit, a meal, and to drop off his laundry, which she'd do for him. In my silence, I marveled that a man who looked half out of his mind, mumbling words that were incoherent to me could be understood by my grandmother. Scatman would know that the word on the street was that he was among the many who could come to Aunt Bea's home for a hot meal and kind words. When he left, Scatman would thank her over and over again, at the door, and again as he walked off. "Thank you, Aunt Bea," he'd mumble as he walked down the sidewalk. "Thank you, Aunt Bea." (She was known as "Aunt Sister Girl" to family and "Aunt Bea" to those who needed a family.)

My grandmother sang while folding laundry in homes of those who weren't very appreciative of her, blessing their homes while humming and singing, always so tenderly respectful of their things. I learned watching her whisper kinds words as prayers while cleaning and polishing the homes of unappreciative "White Folks" she would make Christmas desserts for, because "It's easier to catch more flies with honey than you do with vinegar." She would add, "Hurt people, hurt people. We help them feel better and hope they will do the same for others."

Her words and actions affirmed that there was something inside me that was capable of doing so much more than I might see around me in others, that I was strong even though I was timid. I didn't have to be the loudest, the best, the model in the magazine. I just needed to be me. From her I learned that there's a way to show up and care and love and demonstrate, no matter what you've been through or are going through, where you live — we don't need permission to show up and love people. These are the random acts you don't speak of. You just do them.

Because she was a domestic worker, most people assumed that she had little money and, through things they said and did, condescended to her. She didn't pay any attention to them. When I was twelve, we were cleaning a doctor's apartment. I never understood how this woman, who was dedicated to healing, could be so hurtful to others. One day I was looking at old passports she had on display. She saw me and said, "Those are from my travels around the world. It's too bad you can't do something like that, and that you never will." Then she walked out of the room. My grandmother came right to me, looked me in the eye, and said, "Don't pay her no never mind," the equivalent of saying "just ignore her" or as her great-granddaughter would later say, "You do you, and I'll do me."

Just by being who she was, she created moments that trained my eyes to see what others might miss and to listen closely to the hearts of others by paying attention to what wasn't always being spoken. I would experience an order to my life that would put me in the right places at the right time. The more I grew, the more I longed to experience and share the love of God and watch the multiple ways it was expressed through others. I carried this curiosity and this desire to do two things in particular from a very early age: One of them was to join the Peace Corps and the other was, eventually, to become an exchange student living abroad. The adventure of living abroad begins with an adventure within you.

I encourage you to be on the lookout for the opportunities to observe and create one random act of kindness. Then take a step of action. In so doing, you open your heart and fine-tune your ears to hear what others cannot in their busyness. Be comfortable with who you are and how life orders your steps. Today, reflect on the areas that you may have been falsely believing to be weakness, those "If I were just more like (fill in the blank)" words you may have told yourself or been told by others.

It's my hope and prayer that today you love who you are. One condition: if the words are honestly geared toward making you a better person, then welcome them into your life and see what better paths await you as you exchange one behavior for another, one turn for another.

Songs
OF THE DAY

It's a Man's World
JAMES BROWN WITH LUCIANO PAVAROTTI

Queen of the Night Arias; The Magic Flute (Die Zauberflöte)
WOLFGANG AMADEUS MOZART, SUMI JO

SHIRLEY TEMPLE CURLS AND THE WILL TO DO IT!— SWITZERLAND

"You can't go back and change the beginning, but you can start where you are and change the ending."

C.S. LEWIS

Like millions of little Black girls in the 1960s with 4C hair (the kinkiest of kinky), I spent Saturday mornings sitting by the stove getting my hair pressed. And if it was a special occasion, my mother would take the time to wind my hair into Shirley Temple curls. One Saturday morning, after watching *Heidi* on TV the night before, I sat on a stool, hands cupping my ears to protect them, daydreaming about the Alps, while my mother wound my newly-straightened hair into Heidi-like ringlets. "I used to dream of going to Switzerland too," she whispered. My mother had seen the movie when she was a little girl. Surprised, I forced myself not to turn around to look at her, her past warnings sounding in my head: *Don't move your head, Gael-Sylvia, or you'll get burned.*

"What do you mean?!" I asked.

Our family had been among the thousands who watched the special airing of the movie *Heidi* with Shirley Temple as a Friday evening special event. In the Black community, there were TV shows and movies universally regarded as special occasions. We didn't have the 24-hour access connecting us to voices from the past that we do today. This was a special occasion and Shirley Temple curls and this Black girl's dream of the Alps started in that moment of ear-holding, heat rising from the stove, and the whisper of my mother's voice. Perfect soil for a dream to be planted.

As my mother pressed and curled her Black girl's hair, I witnessed an invisible connection between the curly-haired White girl on TV and my mother. My mother had *dreams?* She had *dreams?!* It was a foreign thought, but I held it, trying to imagine her as a little girl, and as an adult mother, carrying that secret longing in her body. Who would have ever imagined this? The notion belied her day-to-day role and responsibilities as a mother, wife, secretary, laundress, housekeeper, dressmaker, grocery shopper, teacher, baker, neighbor, and participant in numerous community activities.

From that moment on I never saw her in the same way. Within that new thought were the seeds I would quietly carry as my own possibility of making her dream of Switzerland come true through me. The vision, the dream, the pondering of possibilities improved my reading skills as I devoured everything about a place I'd never heard of mentioned in our household. As I observed and listened closely to others my mother's age, I sometimes quietly inquired about the dreams I assumed were most privately held within their little girl selves. Several who were musicians spoke of dreams they'd had of going to college. Others, who like my grandmother made the regular drive to what seemed to me to be far-off places—Baltimore, the cotton fields in Arkansas (my grandmother), and Alabama—to visit family (all places that seemed exotic and far away to me), spoke of dreams of traveling to what felt exciting and different to them, like Hawaii. One woman spoke of being a concert pianist. I didn't remember her ever even owning a piano.

Heidi gave my mother and me something in common—a dream that sparked an insatiable hunger to learn more about others, places they lived, and the dreams they held within. Prompted by *Heidi,* and Shirley Temple's portrayal of the little orphan girl, images of the famous Swiss Alps, the goats that contribute to their famous cheese, Swiss chocolates, hiking in the hills for wild blueberries and the elusive Edelweiss, and baking fresh bread in a Swiss home filled my dreams. The vision was fed by the mailman presenting gifts from afar—stamps and postmarks from my growing number of pen pals from lands I could access only by plane or ship. My curiosity about the world has yet to lessen and my appetite grows with my dreams to see more of the sacred places where others hold the longings of their hearts. As my dear sister-friend Tanya says, "We've walked on water! Why would we ever want to stay in the boat?" She's referring to Matthew 14: 22:31, when Jesus encouraged Peter to get out of the boat he rode in with the other disciples and walk on the water with him, which he did, until fear took over and he started to sink.

Tanya's and my thinking is this: why would you settle for anything less than miraculous? Why stay in the boat? I continue to walk in visions revealed in dreams that become come true.

At times, my few months in Switzerland were my unknowing introduction to life on an island, where I'd later spend my time in the Peace Corps. I was isolated because of my Christian faith and values. I didn't drink, so I was mocked by other American high school exchange students. I didn't wild out, like my two exchange sisters, so although we were friendly, we didn't hang out. I didn't have a boyfriend, which pushed me into silent observation of others sporting "promise rings" and the treasured varsity jackets from their athletic boyfriends. On the flip side, I liked what I learned in school and how I felt reading my Bible. And I enjoyed indulging my curiosity about a different culture, especially accompanying my Swiss mother to her weekly lunch gathering with other stay-at-home mothers, following their grocery shopping routines, though I was the only non-adult present (I'd always been comfortable with any generation) and couldn't understand a word they said.

Before I left the US, I'd begun making new friends from the various neighborhoods that fed my high school, those segregated by affluence and ethnicity—Black, Caucasian, Latino—and with students studying from abroad. All of this integrated our household, and I participated in social activities in their homes, went on beach trips, and joined youth groups on campus to study the Bible.

In Switzerland, my curiosity and appreciation of other ways of being granted me an invitation into the segregated part of Basel where the Turkish gypsies lived. Until I sat down to eat with the gypsies, played with their children, listened to their stories, and learned the songs of their hearts. I didn't know this was a first for them. They hadn't interacted socially with anyone outside their community. And when I got back to my host family, they couldn't understand why I'd wanted to visit with the gypsies. There was no way my host family could see any reason to mingle with the gypsies. And whether the gypsies had the desire or not, they saw no way to reach out and connect with the outside community.

But I had found a way and learned a valuable lesson: making a way out of no way requires being uncomfortable and being open.

Living in Switzerland provided me with the opportunity to make a choice: discard my identity or embrace my difference. I chose to embrace me and be open to learning from others, even in my silence. Having beliefs that differ from others is as much a culture shock as clearing customs in a new homeland. I've lived all over, and it isn't home for me until I can find and make peace with who I am and where I am, regardless of whether I know the language or not.

In the quietness of those lonely homesick moments in Switzerland, I may have felt like I was living on a remote island, but in those moments I also learned that you can't live on a remote island and not learn to embrace silence and the autonomy that comes from being isolated. My faith says that I'm never alone, and I carry my faith wherever I go, whether in the company of the like-minded or isolated from the presence of fellow believers. I do so now, and I did so then.

I returned home with the sure-fire belief that my time in Switzerland had filled me with memories of dreams come true: from picking blueberries to eating my favorite breakfast in a Swiss chalet—homemade *bircher muesli* to accompany the freshly baked bread—to eating Swiss chocolates and buying every souvenir I once gazed upon in that junior high school library. All were treasures that remained beyond the joyless moments, treasures that came with being open to new people, new places, and dreaming big dreams of possibilities.

I learned that I could choose to drown in a sea of tears and self-pity or rise up and look for the good around me and walk, skip, crawl, run, jump, dance to whatever song played in my head, to just sing it and move toward the good. That time in Switzerland was when I learned to live and lead from a place of joy. It was a choice.

I encourage you to be open and try on the joy of discomfort by trying something new. Better still, put yourself in the company of people who live in a world so different from yours that you become the bridge to possibilities in relationships that others may have thought impossible. Start by being your own best friend. Set aside time to spend with yourself—maybe once a week—doing something festive, exploring a new part of the city you live in, whatever interests and excites you. Have fun. Push the limits. Do something that sparks your imagination, a sense of joy, of fun. Play. If it interests you, let these new images, sounds, ideas that stem from this time with yourself inspire and feed your creative projects.

My hope and prayer is that you experience the joy of your own company. Being alone periodically can bring out the small child in us who's afraid of the monsters under the bed when our imaginations run wild in the darkness. Embracing that time with ourselves can cause us to explore, to embrace possibilities, and to grow.

Je T'aime

LARA FABIAN

WHO'S YOUR ACTIVIST?—
GERMANY

*"We hired you for your opinion and the minute
you cease to give it you lose your value."*
CHANNING DUNGEY

"And that's the moment you stop trusting your voice."
GAEL-SYLVIA PULLEN

To live well, I believe you must have a positive mentor and become a positive mentor. Miss Dittus, my seventh-grade teacher, was one of those mentors to me.

Before my first trip away from my family and community, my first time flying in an airplane, my first time outside the United States, I timidly shared with my seventh-grade class my curiosity about living short-term in another country, meeting other families, and going to school there. I had no idea how to achieve my dream, or if it were even possible.

"Gael-Sylvia," Miss Dittus said, "you can! It's called being an exchange student. You can go when you're in high school." Mind you, I was twelve years old and being in high school was as difficult to comprehend as hopping on a plane, yet it sounded right. The potential of learning, seeing, and experiencing life with people from around the world sounded amazing, but how could I do it? How could I afford it? Would my parents allow me to go? I asked all these questions out loud.

That's the thing about a great mentor. Miss Dittus didn't have all the answers, but she planted seeds of hope and a belief in great expectations. Her interest in my softly spoken dream ignited the spark of encouragement we can all use when setting out in new directions. Perhaps because of her sincerely spoken words of encouragement, along with a life of encouragement from my grandmother and father, for the first time I truly felt my own life's value and the possibilities my dreams and musings could open to me.

After class, I asked Miss Dittus where I should begin; she pointed me to the library. When I questioned how would I handle potential homesickness a world away, she inspired me with enthusiastic words to override my doubt and fear: "Gael-Sylvia, can you imagine all the new friends your age you'll make? Can you imagine all the people who will be so happy to share with you? Seeing what the Swiss do in their everyday life? The new music you'll hear? Can you imagine the new tastes you will experience? Can you *imagine?*"

I could, with her help. Within that moment and many more to follow, I learned the necessity of sharing my voice—speaking up, even if it's a whisper. This was 1970, in Pomona, California. The civil rights marches had transitioned into Vietnam War protests, hippies, Sly and the Family Stone, afros, dashikis. And even with all this upheaval and change, *Jet* magazine didn't show people who looked like me traveling to and living in other parts of the world. I'd have to imagine it.

Miss Dittus had told our class many times that "It's hard not to judge people solely by their appearance, but you must try." My parents had taught us the same thing—whether it was skin color, style of dress, or mannerisms. Miss Dittus was Caucasian, of German descent, from South Dakota. Yet she filled us with tales of her world travels to bring the boring parts of geography and English lessons to life, to connect us with those places we read about. Her teaching style was strict and without laughter, in alignment with the tight bun she wore daily, her mouth and nose pinched as tightly as the compression stockings she wore to reduce discomfort from standing all day. All this made her appear unapproachable and closed off. It made her seem different. Yet the excitement, encouragement, and open-mindedness I heard in her words that day contrasted sharply with her outward appearance.

Within that moment before the school bell dismissed us, I felt a warm, non-restrictive open heart which seemed to have been searching, waiting for one of her students to see beyond the text-book, see beyond all that held her within the boundaries of that classroom. In my own way, I wanted to let her know that I saw her too. I lingered after class and then I spoke in my small, still voice, and for the first time, I felt she heard and saw me loud and clear, much louder and clearer than I saw myself. She saw a new world waiting for me and lying within me. Had I not spoken up, that world of possibilities may have been deferred. Fortunately it was, because I shared my heart so openly with her that she was able to speak words of belief into me.

Her eyes sparkled as she smiled. She looked different to me, and I would look at possibilities differently from that point for-ward. I was thankful to have openly shared a part of myself with her. This time, someone saw more potential than I knew existed.

And from that moment, I also saw the difference inspirational dreams can have for others, including an entire community.

There are moments filled with the voices of people speaking hurtful and discouraging words because they have no imagination left and their own dreams have died within. Hurt people, hurt people. It's hard to ignore them and sometimes it takes years before we can see what took root and began to produce its own kind of strange fruit. We may not know what others have imagined or do imagine, but we can encourage them with "Can you imagine...?" We can encourage ourselves.

That was the seed Miss Dittus tucked deep into my heart and mind: imagine. It would be many years later that I would associate a new name for *imagining*: visualizing. Miss Dittus assured me that just as others had found a way, I would too. From then on, I'm sure she and I saw each other differently as I reciprocated her enthusiasm each time she handed me a brochure or an article about foreign exchange students. In other words, my mentor was watering that seed she'd planted.

Eventually, she moved back to Germany and I became a summer exchange student in Switzerland. During that time, we connected for a few days of travel around Germany—me sharing with her the surprises from my summer experiences of staying with a Swiss friend and his family at their summer chalet, hiking the Alps to pick blueberries, and buying cheese from a local dairy farmer to eat with our daily home-baked bread.

My knowledge of Black history deepened as I sat one bright and sunny afternoon on the patio of a busy German restaurant. Miss Dittus had suggested we meet there. It was one of her favorites because of the *schnitzel*, the delicious dish of meat, pounded thin, covered in flour, beaten eggs, and breadcrumbs, then sautéed. We recounted our versions of our history together that had brought us to that moment, my diligence as a pen pal, and why she had returned to her family's homeland. We were adding to our story of friendship in a place filled with special memories for her.

The waiter took her order for Coke and schnitzel, then the manager came to our table and a fierce exchange ensued between Miss Dittus, the waitress, and the manager. Although I didn't understand German, I understood universal body language and tone. I knew their words had something to do with me. It turns out, they wouldn't serve me. Miss Dittus was furious. The blind ignorance and hatred sparked by Hitler's years in power had lingered into the next generation who lived alongside those who also felt shame and remorse. The manager and waitress insisted. Miss Dittus persisted. They pointed at me, and I looked at her, perplexed. They refused to serve a Black person, not even a happy high school one.

Miss Dittus grabbed her purse and walked away briskly. With a peace in me that's hard to explain, I followed. No schnitzel. No Coke. I took one last look back at all the staring faces and felt sad for them.

Later, what I remembered most were two things. First, how outraged Miss Dittus was and that a White lady would be more upset about their treatment of me than I was, me the Black focus of the upset that caused all eyes to turn in our direction. And second, the prayer that ran through my head, *Lord, is this possibly a time I can learn to love through prayer? When I get to pray for someone who's hurting so badly that they can hate with confidence?*

Internally, I spoke words of confidence in my faith in Christ, asking love to heal and for love to prevail. This was my opportunity to look, learn, and understand what the textbooks, Dr. King's speeches, my parents and ministers spoke of: the ugly side of anger and the danger of hate when allowed to fester, the power to love through prayer when no other words would make sense, the power of prayer to do the impossible, make peace. Then I prayed to God of all creation to show me how to love in ways greater than all that's possible, so that hatred would never be planted within me.

Despite this experience filled with hatred and prejudice, my memories of Germany are filled with the kindness of my mentor and sunny days walking together in a dream come true. Upon my departure, Miss Dittus presented me with a cherished Hummel figurine to make up for the bad experience of my not being served at a restaurant because I'm Black. More than forty years later, the figurine sits on my mother's bookshelf. Embracing and believing in the power of possibilities to love bigger, wider, and intentionally is how I learned to lead from a place of joy. When I hear German or see something about Hitler, I don't recall that afternoon; I recall Miss Dittus, someone who encouraged me to believe that no dream is impossible and to hold tightly to mine.

I encourage you to avoid putting limitations on yourself or others. Be open. Be an explorer. Be a pioneer in your thoughts. Seek new paths. Create new tracks.

It's my hope and prayer that you aspire to dream bigger with eyes and heart wide open to see what's possible, even when you don't yet see the clear path to getting there.

Song
OF THE DAY

Sukiyaki
KYU SAKIMOTO

WHY JAPAN?

一期一会 *(One life, one encounter)*

JAPANESE SAYING

Going from Switzerland to Japan didn't compare to the culture shock I experienced when I accompanied my grandmother to clean homes fewer than 6.3 miles from our own. My first time was in high school and I continued through my freshman year in college. I went because I loved being with her and helping her, though she insisted on paying me. That world was so far from mine that I felt like a foreigner in what I once believed was my own backyard. Although homes were larger, driveways longer, swimming pools nicer, the people who lived there struggled with the same things we did, but their struggles were shaped by the presence of wealth and ours were shaped by the lack of it.

This was in the early 1970s. Black and White families shared familiar routines of work, play, grocery shopping, doctors' appointments, laundry, mothers preparing dinner, crying babies, and troubled teens, but the language and look were different. Their children seemed to cry out for help in bigger ways, because big money allows that—more parties, more drinking, more drugs, more shopping, more divorces, less time, less of God. Their parents went to therapy. Ours went to church.

As very young diaper-wearing toddlers, Black children were often trained to recognize a change in the pitch and tone of a voice and in a subtle shift in facial expression to recognize joy, fear, contentment, praise, disappointment, anger. We could tell when all was well and when it wasn't going to go well for us. Public displays of misbehaving provoked a stern look from our parents or other elders. It was advance warning, a heads up, putting us on notice that if we were disrespectful or disobedient, we could anticipate the equivalent of the wrath of God in the form of spankings or harsh tongue-lashings once we were out of public space. If we ignored the subtle signals, then public embarrassment was guaranteed, because disrespect was intolerable and bringing shame upon our parents and families was and unacceptable.

My observation was that White children were given endless chances: "One… Mary, give the book back to your brother. Two… Now, please. Two and a half… How many times do I have to tell you? Three…" And on it went. No consequence named or given. The expressions of love and protection given to us at home were life lessons intended to protect us from societal consequences our ancestors had experienced being Black and not having endless chances.

Our parents would just look at us and whatever was going to happen on the other side of three happened at one. There was no conversation, no counting, only the voice of authority to be respected because it was coming from a place of safety and love. Theirs came from money and optional rewards of plane trips to exotic locations or buying sprees to department stores that boasted family names and street addresses: Saks Fifth Avenue, Joseph Magnin, Bullocks Wilshire. We traveled ten miles to the beach or bought on layaway at J.C. Penney or Sears Roebuck. If a blender broke, a stereo or a TV, they threw it away and bought new. If those items, viewed as precious treasures in our homes, broke, we fixed them.

It was on the other side of the wall between communities that I learned I was from the group of people viewed as working class and apparently in dire need of being lifted up so that I, too, could have a bigger portfolio, a bigger home, and bigger issues. This help came in the form of college scholarships—close-minded thinking cloaked in diversity initiatives, welcoming a handful of us Black and Brown people into their world of higher socio-economic status, White privilege, and the pride associated with pursuing advanced education. All the while reminding us of the honor it was for us to be admitted into these "highly selective institutions of higher education."

After a summer program for incoming Black students, I started my freshman year at Pitzer College, in Claremont, California, a member of the Claremont Colleges, my education funded by scholarships and work study. The scholarships were based on academics and diversity. It was often falsely assumed by White staff and students that to meet the diversity quota, surely the standards for students of color had been lowered. Untrue. So anyone who saw a Black student automatically assumed we all got in with lower GPAs, even when our GPAs were the same or higher. We were completely objectified. Even with the assumed lower GPA, we were welcomed with open arms, but the message was clear: "So happy you're here. We need the diversity." The mask of White liberal racism—the assumption that racial differences are deep and profound, the fascination with studying us, as though we were a different species, was foreign to me, just as it was to my White working-class friends. They were subject to the same otherness, based on false assumptions, and were challenged to find their own voice. They could assimilate. We couldn't. It was during this time that I began to understand Dr. King's words, "Shallow understanding from people of good will is more frustrating than absolute misunderstanding from people of ill will." I had entered a new fight for civil rights and respect.

The value of economic diversity with White middle- and lower-middle-class students wasn't an issue for White faculty, staff, and fellow students. It wasn't obvious that many shared similar backgrounds to the students of color, because externally they blended into the environment, making them unrecognizable and spared by professors who couldn't point them out. But for the rest of us, who were not White and upper middle class, no one was exempt from being the subject of sociological and anthropological case studies used to justify why we were less fortunate than others. Those of us who were considered the less fortunate, those of us being studied, were encouraged to share our thoughts so professors and classes could scrutinize the sociological influences of our upbringing and how best to label the perceived deficiencies that would allow us to forever be the poster children for their future philanthropy. We were the source of their case studies.

This was their training ground and we were their subject. God help us! And such excellent subjects we were if we stayed in the social sciences. Gifted with wisdom, skill, and talent, more than three quarters of my fellow incoming freshman of color opted out of social studies and majored in science and empirical data, areas where numbers rule and high future dollars would prevail. They opted for pre-med, pre-law, and pre-dentistry as majors. They excelled in advanced chemistry. I never did well in advanced math of any kind and had to find my place within social studies.

Interestingly, this was also my introduction as an undeclared sociologist, observing the language, influence, and upbringing of other non-White students whose parents were second- and third-generation wealth, with degrees for post-graduate studies in medicine, law, and chemistry. They were proficient in math. The Chicago-based wealthy parents of two of my roommates were striving to put their names on buildings like the Carnegies and Rockefellers. Most of these students were Black. And though we looked the same, and I believed I should have felt at home with them, I was naively surprised by our differences and learned a lot about myself and expanding my perspective of my own potential. Many of these students had attended prep schools. They had cars and funds to promptly access professional Black beauticians, freeing them to swim without worrying about their hair. They were girls who were as comfortable as their White roommates leaving their scent on expensive bars of soap their parents purchased from the same department stores. They also had their own cars! They came from neighborhoods I assumed were filled with large homes and long driveways, because I would hear others whisper whenever their backs were turned during BSU (Black Student Union) gatherings.

Some of these girls were graduates of celebrity-status private and public schools, such as Beverly Hills High School. They benefited from assimilation into White America because of Black networks that discriminately provided exposure and opportunities not available to all Black people. They spoke of being second- and third-generation members of Jack 'n Jill, an elite organization for

"America's Black upper class," whose members include many of the first Black millionaires, politicians, and generations of prominent Black families.

Other than reading about people with these backgrounds in *Ebony Magazine* or accompanying my father to the barbershop and reading *Jet*, I had never been up close and personal with any of them. I saw all Black people as being the same—as long as we were all members of the NAACP, liked Motown, and fought for civil rights. Nothing would seem unusual about a group that was selective in its membership. After all, my own parents were members of the Freemasons and Eastern stars, until my mother decided that being segregated within the already segregated Black community wasn't for her. All societies have specific requirements for members and reserve the right to exclude certain populations. She modeled for us that this segregation wasn't for her, and thus not for us either.

These wealthy Black girls didn't grow up like many of my friends, as Girls Scouts, but they were cool and smart and they, too, forced my mind to be open to another world of possibilities that comes with being in this Black girl skin, with Black girl hair and Black girl dreams. I didn't understand their lifestyles and values, but we shared other things in common. We were at this college for a world of possibilities.

Yet still, I felt I didn't belong. *What's going on?* I kept asking myself. *I should feel at home here.* I could ride my bike to school. I was that close. So feeling like a foreigner in this domestic environment, I decided it might easier to be me and understand others if I saw more of the world. So I went to Japan for my sophomore year, even though that option to study abroad was reserved for juniors.

By nature I'm an engaging introvert, an observer, and a selective participant, but at that time, I became lost in the conflicting messages and haunting introductions to Black- and Brown-skinned people who lost themselves within their advanced education. They lost the soul of their heart by drinking the Kool-Aid that limited intelligence, value, and culture based solely on Anglo-Saxon American standards. The message was clear: "You've come to this side of the wall to be like us." So they complied. They started straightening their hair, talking differently, carrying themselves differently. They forgot who they were, where they came from. They bought into the belief that you aren't of value if you didn't come from those with the same high income and academic aspirations. So, they set out to become of value. They got into positions as academic heads, and totally lost their soul and their hearts. I was experiencing the double consciousness that W.E.B. Du Bois wrote of in 1903, in *The Souls of Black Folk*, and witnessing the idea that Black people must have two fields of vision at all times. We must be conscious of how we view ourselves, as well as being conscious of how the world views us.

The subliminal messages of objectification caused me to question myself: *Who am I? Where do I belong?* And so I went to Japan to find out.

I hadn't studied Japanese. But I had a strong desire, fed partially by memories of family friends visiting our home from a place called Japan. I was in elementary school at the time. The wife was from Japan, her in-laws from Mexico and Indiana. Their children spoke Japanese and Spanish, but their hair looked like ours and that of their father, who was African-American and Hispanic. They kind of looked like me, but they spoke other languages and offered treats and gifts from their mother's homeland. The seed was planted. Japan? Mexico? Africa? One family, in a single day, confirmed what I would later come to know as true: we're all connected. *How can this be?* I thought at the time.

Never mind that I didn't know the language, the people, or the culture, had never tasted the food, or didn't know how to maneuver chopsticks. I wanted to go. Growing up, I'd also had a burning desire to understand the emotion, place, culture behind the song *Sukiyaki* by Kyu Sakamoto, his rich, mournful, oddly upbeat voice blasting from the AM radio station we listened to as we ate our oatmeal before school. One image of family friends, one song, and one new calling: Go to Japan. Never mind that I didn't meet the strict stipulations of being a junior in college.

Never mind that the only thing I knew about Japan was from reading books and deciding to organize an international day at my high school. Two years earlier, still in high school, I'd decided to ask my gym teacher, Miss Tanaka, for input about Japan. She agreed to tell me what seaweed was and to bring samples of sushi from her "real Japanese" friends after getting over being offended that I would label her as "Japanese" just because her parents were from Japan and her last name was Tanaka, when, as she put it, "I'm from Diamond Bar! I don't know anything about Japan. I'll ask my real Japanese uncle and his friends." She may have lost her Japanese identity, but I would find mine.

As fate would have it, my freshman year roommate was a Japanese-Hawaiian girl from an elite private college girls prep school. Another was Japanese-Hawaiian from another private prestigious Hawaiian prep-school. I watched and learned, perhaps marveled, at how easily they could ebb and flow between multiple groups of the same economic background. Their comfort and common experiences with Jewish girls from similar private girls' schools belied the generational challenges their parents and grandparents experienced, experiences which were on par with many of us who were from the Black and Latino public schools.

Up to that point in life, our worlds couldn't have been more different. My high-school grad night had been to Disneyland. My Japanese-Hawaiian roommate's graduation had been a trip to Japan to learn more about her parents' background, a sort of field study between prep school and college. We learned from one another as we expanded our world of relationships and experiences that freshman year. I just had to go. It was the first time a verse from the Bible — "The LORD appeared to Isaac and said, 'Do not go down to Egypt; live in the land where I tell you to live'" (Genesis 26:2) — reaffirmed a calling. I had this verse pinned to my bulletin board. Although these words were spoken to Isaac, it was my non-Christian roommate who pointed out, "Doesn't that say, 'live in the land where I tell you to live'? Why won't you, Gael-Sylvia, go to Japan, a new land, and live there?" She meant that there were bigger place to go to experience different opportunities. God encouraged Isaac, and that's what she was doing for me. Hearing her question provided the answer I needed. There was no further fear, no more conversation. I decided to go to Japan. Once again, there was only the voice of Authority to be respected because it was coming from a place of safety, faith, and love. And, she had been watching and listening to me in ways I had not been aware of.

Perhaps it was my impassioned essay, naivete, or bold audacity to ask, but I was approved by the colleges—at home and in Japan —to go my sophomore year. To this day, going to Japan remains the most pivotal moment of my life and its influence was beyond my wildest dreams, affecting generations to come, families that had yet to be birthed from marriages that hadn't yet happened.

I had the honor of living with the Uehatas, who were in their sixties, when they opened their home to me and five other foreign exchange students. They were a somewhat non-traditional host family, twice the age of most. They were also one of the wealthiest families in Japan, living in one of the wealthiest communities in the region, if not the country: Seijogakuen-mae on the Odakyu Line. The wealth I was exposed to cleaning homes with my grandmother and the privilege I saw at Pitzer were nothing compared to what the Uehatas had.

There were several houses on their property. The Uehatas lived in the big house, a non-traditional palatial home. The other students and I had our daily interactions on the first floor of their house, but we never saw the second or third stories of their home. A duplex housed their middle son and his family on one floor and another foreign student on the second. Another duplex was home to their youngest son and his family who lived on one floor, and two exchange students who lived on another. And a third unit was where I lived with three more foreign students—a blend of a semi-traditional Japanese-style home with tatami mats and western beds. The entire compound was hidden behind towering concrete walls in a neighborhood of low-rise bamboo fences.

They may have lived behind concrete walls, but they opened their home and lives to me and others. Not only had they invited six exchange students into their home and their lives, but they also allowed me to invite others from around the world, students at school—people I met while exploring the city—inside the walls they'd built internally and externally.

Inviting multiple strangers into their home was a foreign concept to most in Japan. It wasn't a familiar part of their culture. And for those who were senior citizens, like the Uehatas, it was even more rare. But the Uehatas welcomed us and all the responsibilities of having college-age young adults living under their roof. I'm not sure why they decided to open their home, but I do know they were curious, as I was, and I know I intrigued them. Everything was new for me. *I* was new to me. And unlike my reaction to those who put me under the microscope at Pitzer, I embraced their curiosity, because it came from a place of sincerity rather than analysis. Their generosity opened my eyes and heart. It amazed me that I was so far from my family, in an environment that couldn't be more different from what I knew, and I felt so completely at home.

Not unlike my travels to Switzerland and Claremont, it didn't take long for me to realize that my upbringing was different from that of other girls—the girls from Pitzer, my fellow exchange students, the girls raised in Japan. Growing up in an environment where others made assumptions about who I was, I was raised to understand that wherever I was, it was absolutely okay to be me, even if people found me difficult to understand. My Japanese host father said, again and again, "Gael-san, don't talk to strangers. Japanese girls don't talk to strangers. Japanese girls don't meet people on the train and invite them home for dinner. You must be properly introduced."

One minute Mrs. Uehata would be smiling with approval while Kyung, the Korean-American roommate, practiced Chopin on the grand piano and the next, smile wiped from her face, she'd leave the room mumbling under her breath, house slippers echoing as she dragged herself through the concert-size rooms, weary from repeating to me, "Japanese girls don't do this, Gael-san. Japanese girls don't do that." All I had done was smile and talk to strangers, inviting them home for dinner, conversation, and out dancing with me and others. I'm friendly like that. It's not a bad thing. I believe that every encounter is a once-in-a-lifetime encounter. Think of how many first-and-only-time events, people, and opportunities occur in the day-to-day. That said, at first this attitude and my friendliness constantly got me in trouble with the Uehatas.

One day, I caught everyone by surprise, including myself, when I heard myself say in the same manner a soft-spoken intro-verted Black Christian girl would say, which to their ears probably sounded just like a soft-spoken Japanese girl being cautiously polite: "But I'm not Japanese." That was it. That was the turning point toward a new North in my life, no matter where I lived or with whom. I could be *with* them, the Uehatas and others, but not *of* them, and still all could be well with my life, and with my soul. It was a turning point for them, as well. They embraced my odd behavior and welcomed everyone with open arms. When it came time for me to return to the US, they threw a Sayonara party, filling their home with people, music, and food from around the world. They even gave me a hug instead of the formal Japanese bow. They couldn't help but show their smiles.

Within those walls I was reminded, once again, that it's both okay to just be myself and to embrace the beauty of my own di-verse experiences. Everything was new for me. *I* was new to me, and I was curious. I hadn't come to Japan to become Japanese. I'd come to learn more about the world and life beyond my own walls.

I loved interacting with the mix of people who lived behind those concrete walls, the exchange students the Uehatas took in. Some left. New ones came. We slept there, had friends over, studied, and lived semi-independently. During that year, our group dwindled. Two of my housemates left early on because they wanted a "real traditional" Japanese family experience. I stayed because I was having a real inter-cultural, inter-socio-economic, and inter-generational Japanese experience. I got along well with the younger Uehatas. The middle son, his wife, and two young children liked having me recreate American traditions for them to experience, such as a Fourth of July picnic-style barbeque complete with three-legged races, or in October, bobbing for apples and baking apple pie. Another of my housemates had been college roommates with one of Princess Grace Kelly's daughters. We couldn't have been more different, yet we also connected. In one of the classes we shared, it was me she referenced when a bewildered Japanese professor yelled at her in Japanese in front of the entire class: "I just don't understand you!" With rich-girl Korean calm, she said, "Ask Gael-san. She does." Lord, help me!

Then there was the non-traditional thirty-something exchange student, Basha, who rocked her fierce Jewish afro with attitude and was equally fluent in the Japanese language as she was in its feminist and LGBT subculture, daring anyone in any language to question her non-Japanese feminist views. She left. She wanted to experience "the real Japan" and abruptly moved out to reside in the Japanese LGBT subculture.

Another exchange student, a Japanese-American girl, had roots fused and deeply watered by the disparities of South-Central Los Angeles's Black/Latino/Asian community. Since she'd entered the University of Southern California, she'd been trying to climb to the other side of the wall. She wanted out of the ghetto, to completely disassociate herself with all things hood, except for the music, the bodaciousness, and the attitude. She brought all three with her to Japan, along with her drive to swap out the old her from the poorer side of the tracks, where Rodeo Drive was pronounced *Row-dee-o* Drive, for the new her on the side where it was pronounced *Ro-day-o*.

Her plan was to return from Japan as a new version of herself, as a qualified member of her USC sorority house, as the upscale Japanese-girl version who would score a rich doctor one day. She was outright militant about it, unapologetic, daring anyone to question the validity of her choices. And no one did, at least not to her face. Eventually, she married the doctor. They were miserable. Life behind the walls of her home off the wealthy Rodeo Drive didn't work out any different from how it had at the Uehatas. She wasn't a Japanese-Japanese girl. She was an Asian/Black/Latina in a Japanese-American girl body, wearing clothing purchased on Rodeo Drive, attempting to cover up the scars from the rough streets of South Central Los Angeles. Needless to say, she and the Uehatas parted ways. I assume it was because her smoking, drinking, and cussing weren't how Japanese girls were supposed to act. They had so many high hopes for her as a Japanese (American) girl. They expected that she would teach me and the Korean girl how to not be so... well, us. That didn't work out.

Then there was exchange student who from Australia who wore a winter coat made from real kangaroo hide, hair intact. She was loud and rude, and made no secret of her distaste for Japanese food, which taught me to always be appreciative of others' hospitality. However much attention she drew with her Aussie accent and kangaroo coat, she received less attention at the train station than I did in my coat of faux snakeskin. "*Sugoi-ne,*" (which can mean amazing, terrible, or bizarre, sometimes all three at once), they'd say as they stared in disbelief, pointed, and backed out of the way. "Sugoi-ne." I don't know if the snakeskin had some symbolism or it was the sight of a Black girl wearing that odd coat.

Whatever reason, they jumped back and parted, giving us a wide birth as we carried our books and burdens home at the end of each school day, which made it easy for us to find a seat on the crowded train.

That roommate didn't last long either. She felt uncomfortable being different and frequently asked, "How many more days until I can go back home?" They finally responded, "*Ashita*. Tomorrow!" As we waved goodbye to her taxi, Kyung and I mimicked the Uehatas' deep bowing, hands resting crossed on our thighs, looking toward the ground. Once the gate to the concrete wall was closed and secured, we saw the Uehata's conservative version of Snoopy's happy dance. Everyone burst out laughing with relief. Laughter entered the home that day.

It was, however, the post-graduate student, the Quaker girl, Susan, from Lincoln, Pennsylvania, and I who ending up staying the full year with the Uehatas. Susan was living in Japan because of a very special history and tradition with the Emperor. We became sisters, and she's been a part of my life ever since. Her open heart and Pennsylvania Dutch accent intrigued me as much as her fluency and knowledge in all things from Negro history to Black history and how she could share it in Japanese. She knew the hearts of our stories because both her parents and grandparents lived it. Descendants of the Quakers who made the Underground Railroad a reality, she'd embarked on a lifelong journey to inform, engage, and educate others about true civil rights.

The three of us—the Quaker, the Korean, and me—would sit for hours practicing our Japanese writing, speaking, and other studies at the apron hem of our surrogate mother, Mrs. Uehata. Our desire to soak up as much as possible from the inter-generational household that the Uehatas family shared with all of us penetrated the walls that had been built long ago. We experienced a real Japanese family and all that we had in common, even if the lengths of our driveways were different lengths, we spoke different languages, and the income and educational levels were at extreme ends of the spectrum.

And that's why Japan. I learned that we can feel at home anywhere as long as we feel at home in our own skin. And we can take that skin any place in the world and find opportunities to grow, and to create joy, even in those joyless moments. Japan opened my eyes and heart and brought me home to myself. I was able to return to Claremont and look at the people there with love.

I encourage you to look at who lives inside your walls and what makes you feel comfortable and at home. Do the same by taking a peek over that wall and see who and what you could be open to exploring, if you just show up as you and know that a better you can come forth if you are open, gracious, and comfortable in your own skin.

My hope and prayer for you is that wherever you are right now, your presence is a joyful source of laughter, and an invitation to new friendships.

If I Could Build My Whole World Around You

TAMMY TERRILL, MARVIN GAYE

THE LANGUAGE OF
DREAMS—HONIARA,
SOLOMON ISLANDS

*"If you can't fly then run, if you can't run then walk,
if you can't walk then crawl, but whatever you do
you have to keep moving forward."*

REV. MARTIN LUTHER KING, JR.

I'd dreamed about being in the Peace Corps since I was a young
girl flooded with stories of the civil rights movement at home
and a war in a far-off place called Vietnam. I'd sit on the toilet
lid, watching my father shave and apply Noxzema to his skin, as
I breathed in the familiar scent listening to KRLA broadcasting
news from my brother's AM transistor radio. I'd interrupt the
broadcast to ask my father questions about the war: "Why did
people from our neighborhood go and you didn't?" "Where did
they go?" "Where's Vietnam?" "Why would we fight and hurt
other people's families and how does doing that help families like
ours?" When my friends' brothers were drafted, I came home with
more questions. I asked him questions, too, as Walter Cronkite

narrated over black-and-white images of Black and White people fighting at home, and Black, White, and Asian fighting overseas. I wanted to know about these people who were hurting. I wanted to understand.

I carried that dream for a very long time. It stayed with me even when I experienced the ups and downs associated with having other dreams come true—Switzerland, Japan, graduating from college. Each experience had been filled with the experiences I associate with my "Only My God!" faith stories of amazing encounters, adventures, and rich experiences.

And then I went to the Solomon Islands. By the time I landed in this dream-come-true as a Peace Corps volunteer, the war in Southeast Asia had ended. What I didn't realize at the time was that the Solomon Islands, located in the South Pacific, had a recent history of war. They'd been a strategic part of World War II. The campaign began with the Japanese landings and occupation of several areas in the British Solomon Islands and Bougainville, in the Territory of New Guinea, where they launched a surprise attack during the first six months of 1942. Remnants of those battles were everywhere—undetonated grenades from WWII hiding under the lush greenery in the jungle, the sunken ships, fallen planes, and Japanese war treasure buried beneath the bright blue water that drew scores of tourists armed with scuba gear.

I arrived in 1978, only months after the country celebrated its independence from England. I landed for training in the capital city of Honiara, on the island of Guadalcanal, one of the six major islands. I was twenty-three-years old. Upon arriving in Honiara, I was intrigued by how familiar and foreign the modern society of the Solomon Islands felt. Honiara had cars, shops, dirt roads that filled at night with toads, one theatre, and a Chinese restaurant. People called the islands paradise, with its palm trees, bright sunlight, and beautiful Brown people. But I didn't see it that way. I was the first Black Peace Corps volunteer to be stationed there. That meant something to people. A lot of eyes were on me. The people were tremendously warm and greeted me with open arms. Yet a battle started brewing within me from the moment I set foot on the island. Something didn't feel right, but I couldn't pinpoint the source of my unease. Maybe it was the echoes of the recent war still present on those islands. That and a premonition of things to come that I should have listened to but couldn't because this was my *dream*. And because so many were expecting so much from me.

I felt guilty feeling anything other than thrilled to be there. I tried to disguise my inexplicable discomfort with outward happiness, while inwardly forcing contentment. I willed myself to embrace the extremely different yet beautiful environment and tremendously kind people. I faked excitement, even though I had no external reason not to feel that way. The Solomon Islands is like Hawaii times ten. It's the poster for paradise—sunny skies, azure ocean, coral reefs, swaying palms, golden beaches, so much beauty.

I lived and worked among the Melanesian people. During all my travels, this was the first time that people's skin had the same amount of melanin as mine. They were Black like me, but distinctly Melanesian with their blond curly hair. We looked so much alike, but we were so different. Little could I know that this lesson would be repeated years later when my husband and I lived in Cleveland and immersed ourselves in a Black community very different from the one I'd grown up in (I tell that story later in the book): we may look familiar given the color of our skin, but we are unique, and our cultures are very different.

During the training, I roomed with three wonderful strangers from the US, a husband and wife, Janie and James. and a single man, Dennis. It was from them that I learned about those in my country who celebrated the night Dr. King was assassinated. Their relatives had boycotted integration, supported lynching, and caused my grandparents' families to flee north and west. My eyes and heart were open. Theirs were too. None of us would take the limited experiences of those we loved as the final answer to all that's wrong in the world, a solution to "those people" who are different from us. Halfway around the world, people from different worlds in the same country, we connected, sharing a history born of a desire to love and serve others. Amazing grace.

For two months we trained together, sharing meals, language, history, and cultural instruction. We explored our new surroundings on land and by sea. We got through. Janie and James had each other to hold on to. I held on to the thread of a silver lining, trying to understand this long-awaited dream that was hard for me to make sense of. And Dennis held fast to his intrigue at the ghostly images of Melanesian men perched in the Meliaceae trees, who often startled us. I called these men who cooled themselves in the shade of these massive mahogany trees "ghosts." These men fueled his competitive nature, his desire to prove that he could fit in, be like them.

Dennis challenged our language instructor, Isaac, to race to the top of a coconut tree. Keep in mind, in the tropics, a *dwarf* coconut palm can grow twenty to sixty feet tall, and a tall coconut palm can reach ninety-eight feet, taller than a seven-story building! To keep Dennis's pride in check, our teacher, who proved more mature than Dennis, reluctantly agreed to his challenge to climb a dwarf coconut tree. Dennis had been observing and attempting the climb on his own, but never made it all the way to the top.

The instructor climbed one tree with ease. Dennis selected another, one of the taller dwarf trees. This time he made it. We could see his pale sweaty skin at the top of the tree. He tossed green coconut fruit to down to each of us, and we broke out in applause. Dennis—a happy, easy-going, fun guy—was smiling as bright as the sun. The applause hushed as we waited for him to inch his way down to safety. He started and stopped, lingering long after Isaac had landed. We called out. He clung tightly to the trunk. The other men began cutting tentacles from the branches of nearby trees and wrapping them around their waists, to help him if necessary. Janie and I clung to one another trying to understand what was happening. James screamed up to Dennis to "Hold on. Don't let go." Dennis held on for dear life (had he let go he would have fallen to his death), and we held our breath, as he slid, shirtless, in shorts, down the tree, the rough bark scraping raw his pale white skin, exposing muscle and tissue, until our breath whooshed from our lungs, as he collapsed bleeding to the ground.

No ambulances. No hospital nearby. The heat, the humidity, the pain were reminders that we were as green and unfamiliar with our surroundings as all the coconuts lying on the ground surrounding Dennis. It took days for him to recover. I still can't look at a coconut tree without thinking about Dennis and how I prayed as we watched him fight a feverish infection resulting from his severe cuts. After we left for our assignments as healthcare educators in the outer islands, I never heard from him again (I didn't hear from James and Janie either). I never found out if Dennis stayed his full Peace Corps term of two years or not. But this I knew: both of us returned home with scars.

Near the end of our training, prior to each of us leaving for our separate outer island assignments, we were all invited to be a part of the ritual for the graduating high school students at a nearby school. Dennis had recovered enough to attend. We welcomed the distraction from weeks of fearing for Dennis's life. We were so excited. This would be a chance to meet more locals and be introduced to a new experience. We made our way through the beaten path, following the voices of singing teenagers—a beautiful sound that added to my music memories traveling straight from their hearts to my bones. But nothing in my past had prepared me to see smiling teenagers dissecting a full-grown cow. Lord help me! I thought I was going to faint. They laughed and waved. Dennis, Janie, and James ran to join in. I excused myself under the pretense of returning home to get something I left on the bed, but really planning to wait to return until the smell of the grilled and pit-roasted meat, rather than the smell of fresh blood, mixed with the strains of the music.

Let me put this experience in perspective. These were high school students who'd captured and were butchering a cow for the feast. I wasn't so far removed from being a high school graduate myself, but I had never in my life met a graduate of any level of education who could capture and butcher a whole cow. In my experience, beef came in specific cuts wrapped in pink paper and handed over a high counter, where, when I was little, I saw only the butcher's hairy arms handing the package to my grandmother.

After living in Japan, I'd declared myself a lacto-ovo vegetarian, meaning I included eggs and dairy in my vegetarian diet. Truth be told, I'd started eating mostly vegetarian back in high school when I earned bonus points in science class for bringing in sheep eyeballs to be dissected. I got the eyeballs from the same butcher I'd visited with my grandmother. He was a round Italian man with a booming voice. "Are you planning on becoming a doctor?" he asked, striding out from behind the counter in a blood-soaked white apron, carrying the eyeballs in front of him—not wrapped neatly in pink paper but floating in pink-tinged liquid in a clear plastic bag. Everyone turned to watch as the butcher placed the bag in my hands and laughed as my father tried to hold me up as my knees buckled. "These are perfect," the butcher said. "You can see how the lenses are attached."

In most cases, we were reminded of our protein source by a label and the bit of blood we rinsed off after discarding the Saran wrap and yellow Styrofoam packaging it came in, before cubing and searing the meat for beef stew, seasoning and placing it in roasting pans, or shaking it in a brown paper bag with seasoning and flour before dropping it into fat sizzling in the frying pan.

I wanted to allow plenty of time for the high-schoolers' meat to cook, so instead of taking the short cut through the jungle, I trudged alone on the longer dirt road that ran along the outer periphery of the farm and fields of the boarding school. The road was separated from the fields by a bamboo fence designed to keep the sheep and goats from wandering into the surrounding dense vegetation or the distant open field beyond.

We'd walked this road many times in hopes of finding a cab to save us from the humidity and heat by day and the toads at night. So when a cab came from behind me, unsolicited and unnecessary, I innocently waved it along, and once it passed, I turned my thoughts inward once again, eyes on the road. Then I heard the whine of the car driving in reverse, stopping behind me, and shifting into first, the rubber tires crushing dried toads and rock as it drove toward me. I looked up, mindlessly watching as it came closer, faster and recklessly, spewing dirt and dust, until I realized

I wasn't safe. It was coming toward me so close and so fast I didn't know how to react.

It happened so fast. I'd just seen a cow split open and hands ripping the entrails from its gut. When I started down this road, my mind had shut down, I'd felt nauseated, and it hadn't quite occurred to me that the road might not be safe. In retrospect, I rewind and reverse my decision to walk home alone in the bright sunlight of paradise, but I'm not sure what I would have done differently. If I'd taken the dense jungle path, I would have run the risk of setting off a grenade. I'd heard them go off.

The cab tried to block me on the side of the road with the fence. I was hemmed in, choked by the dust, unable to see the cab clearly. The passenger door flew open. Two arms grabbed me with unexpected force. The cab started moving forward as someone else reached around those arms and tugged on my hair. They were dragging me along the road, trying to pull me into the cab. I knew what would happen if they did. I'd heard stories of rape and abduction. I kicked and screamed. They pulled. I struggled. The driver yelled to them to hurry up. I pleaded to him for help. The man holding my hair ripped the cotton straps of my newly-sewn version of an island party dress. I gripped the door frame with all my strength. The dust started to clear, and I smelled the stink of alcohol on the two men's breath, looked into their unfocused eyes. They were drunk. I heard their voices, really heard them. They were yelling at me in Japanese. I'd spent a year in Japan where I had always felt bigger than everybody. I was bigger than these men. No way was I going to let two drunken fishermen take me. I may have looked the part, but I was no quiet island girl. I yelled back. " 行かせて。私を家に帰らせて, *Ika sete. Watashi o ie ni kaera sete!*" "Let me! Let me go home!" My voice was stern, deep and commanding, a voice I'd never heard come forth from me. I don't know where it came from. I felt God with me. I always feel Him with me.

Maybe it was seeing the presence of God or witnessing a Black girl yelling back in their language that shook them to sobriety long enough to drop me. I lay face down on the road—dirt, sand, dried eyes of toads—trying to get my bearings. I had to move. I pushed myself up and ran screaming across the road, across the field, racing full out toward the headmaster's house, even though they were all at the festivities.

The car followed me, close on my heels, until three people came running in my direction — two ghost men sitting in the branches of a majestic Meliaceae had heard my cries for help, and the headmaster, who had stopped by to retrieve last-minute party supplies and seen dust kicking up in the field from a car off the beaten path.

Needless to say, I missed the graduation party. I had survived a kidnapping and rape attempt, and by, of all people, drunken Okinawan fishermen in a blue taxi driven by a Solomon Islander. The Japanese Fisheries Corporation hired Okinawan fishermen from the island of Miyako to carry out fishery operations for branches based in the Solomon Islands. These expats, stranded in isolated outposts of the Solomon Islands, were apparently a notorious part of the island's hidden history—known for their drunken, disruptive behavior. The police and the Peace Corps Director and his wife stared in bewilderment when I told them at the police station that I'd yelled in Japanese at the men.

I didn't know it then, but the beauty of paradise held other opportunities when I wanted to yell "Let me go home!" During my brief time on the islands, there were so many times I wanted to admit I should just go home, but I couldn't. I felt I'd be letting everyone—including myself—down. Instead, I continued to push my feelings deeper down my throat and kept them sealed there, like the grenades in the dense jungles. I was determined to find the joy in my dream, when I knew that what would have truly brought me joy was to go home.

At the police station, I described the men in detail, including the look in their startled eyes that a Solomon Island-looking girl spoke their language. Their insobriety caused them to choose the *wrong* victim. Of all the girls they could have grabbed that day, they made a mistake choosing me. I told them how the men let my arms slip out of their grip, leaving me on the toad-covered dirt road. I told them how students from the neighboring school got word and ran to my rescue, and that the school principal rang the authorities. There are benefits to living on an island if you're trying to catch criminals. There's nowhere to go. It was easy to track down intoxicated Okinawan fishermen in a blue taxi on an island. My point is quite simply that there are times in life when the only thing we want to do is survive. Even in trying circumstances, we want to survive emotionally, stay spiritually grounded, and remain optimistic long enough to get through challenges.

I encourage you to learn another language. Not just in case of an emergency, but for the experience of surprising yourself at how much more you are capable of doing, the places it will take you, and how it can give you a fresh perspective on describing details that one language is insufficient to capture.

It's my hope and prayer that you will know that there is another voice within you. No matter your age, start now to fill yourself with words that you can grab hold of, even if it's in another language, so that when life makes you so uncomfortable you feel weak in the knees, you can speak up for yourself — even if all eyes are upon you. The challenges pass, but the lessons learned stay with you for a lifetime.

Japanese Blues
JEROME WHITE

YOU JUST KIND OF GET
A FEELING—SIOTA

"Inspiration should never be expensive..."

**RACHEL KENNEDY (NATALIE KNEPP),
HALLMARK'S *A JOYOUS CHRISTMAS***

After two months of training in Honiara, we sailed on to our
outer-island assignments. I was assigned to the Siota region
on the island of Ngella Pile, one of the four larger islands in the
Ngella island group, just north of Guadalcanal, where I'd be a
healthcare educator in a local school. My internal discomfort continued. We traveled by canoe to get to Siota from the neighboring
larger island of Guadalcanal. The unfortunate part was that I was
sent there when school wasn't in session, so there were only five people on the school grounds, which meant five people on that entire
side of the island: the grounds keeper and his wife, whose names I
can't remember, the Peace Corps volunteer Stan, whom I was going to be replacing, and his two American visitors, Phil and Lisa.

The presence of the Americans should have helped my
homesickness, but instead they added to it. They were from

Southern California—one from a city near the Orange County beach community, where I live even now as I write this chapter, and the other from Big Bear, a nearby mountain community where I used to hang out growing up. Their excitement about getting off the island and going back home soon just made me miss my home even more. I had dreamed of being in the Peace Corps for a long time, so how could I be homesick?

While Siota was only an island away from Guadalcanal, it had not adopted the British influences but preserved the heritage of generational lifestyles. They were fishermen, basket weavers, healers, and resources of knowledge of living with the earth. Isolated, without the children to engage with, my work yet to begin, I waited with great expectation for word from beyond, supplies, and mail to fuel my dreams of home.

On my second day, Stan, Phil, Lisa, and I walked through the jungle to the native village on the other side of the island. I'd heard the inhabitants had once practiced cannibalism. Every Solomon Islander who'd learned of my assignment to Siota had gotten a kick out of trying to scare me with that vital piece of information. While the villagers may have left cannibalism behind, everything else was frozen in time—the thatched huts constructed of tree palms, the men in sarongs only, the women and girls with vibrant red hibiscus flowers woven in their curly blond hair, wearing only skirts made of earthy root fibers mixed with long wild grass.

I smiled as I watched the happy, laughing children running and playing, their toughened bare feet stamping the earth, the azure ocean surrounding them. All of this was both beautiful and perplexing. Familiar and foreign. They were at home. I wasn't. They worked and lived off the natural provisions of the sea and land. They were warm and friendly, as was I, and we stared at one another, probably thinking similar thoughts of familiarity and differences. With our dark skin, we looked very similar, but we were different. Their curly hair was blonde and wild. My curly hair was black and braided. Inside, I struggled to hold it together, afraid of unravelling, going wild, like my tightly twisted hair would look in a few weeks if not properly managed. *Hold it together, Gael-Sylvia.* I would have to hold it together and manage my jumble of emotions over the next two years.

The nights were harder, especially because I lacked appreciation for the home-brewed hibiscus wine that intoxicated the group I was with and the people from the other side of the island who were waiting for their ship home. They sat around drinking, telling stories of how fast they would run to the nearest airplane, all while assuring me, "Gael-Sylvia, you'll love it here," and trying to get me excited about what it would be like when the kids came back from break: "Everyone has been waiting for you to arrive, well, they were before they left on a long break. They'll be so excited to see you when they get back."

But it didn't matter how much they encouraged me; I just couldn't get used to living on a small island, in a small country that had just gained its independence, where all the people knew my name. I waited for the place to grow on me, but it didn't. The feeling of unease continued. I was constantly being told that I was living in paradise. I tried to believe it and make it so. I didn't know then, but the island life would draw me closer to God.

The effects of World War II showed up in a variety of ways in Siota. Now and then I'd hear the random grenades exploding, sometimes causing tragic losses of lives to unsuspecting children playing in the jungle or adults clearing the bush to make paths. Then there were the structures that were remnants from the war—

Western-style dormitories and concrete structures with poor ventilation. I'd been assigned to an entire dormitory by myself. It was nearly unbearably hot and stuffy. I would have preferred a hut, with its better ventilation.

On my second night staying in the overheated dorm room, my constant brushing at something on my face and neck woke me up. It was more than the wind blowing through the open window. My skin felt like it was crawling, the tingling sensation of pins and needles firing randomly on my nose, my ear, my chest. Barely awake, annoyed by having my dreams disturbed, I switched on the small lamp on my nightstand. By the dim light, I could see some movement, but nothing more. Slinging back the sarong I used as a sheet, I groped for the switch on the wall to turn on the overhead light. The illumination sent huge insects resembling what we in America would think was a mix between a giant ugly water bug and a cockroach (I'm not sure which they were) scattering across the bed, my sarong, the sheet and pillow, all of them searching frantically, as most malevolent spirits do when faced with the light, for dark spaces to hide. I was covered in bugs! I jumped off the bed, spinning, shaking, swiping the insects out of my braided hair, from my ears, off my back, dropping to my knees and swatting at them. I muffled screams, but I couldn't hold back the tears.

I got up off the insect-covered bed, huddled in a corner on a mat, on the cool floor and freaked out in the privacy of paradise. Overwhelmed by the sense of isolation, frightened by the creepy sensation that filled me when I thought about being there for two long years, I stayed in the corner of the room until sunlight, trying to make sure I was no longer covered by insects. Afraid to move, wiping at my tears, hugging my cassette player to me and singing with my favorite songs until dawn, I tried not to cry. I was still living the dream, right? That's what I told myself hoping to soothe myself throughout the dark hours. I tried to "be strong and of good courage," just as I'd read and heard about through the many years of sermons, Bible studies, and Sunday School lessons, rationalizing that perhaps this was a moment in my life to apply what I'd learned. I had no life references to guide me in this situation.

The next morning, covered with welts and bumps, eyes red and puffy from crying (I lost that battle), I set off to join the others for breakfast at Stan's hut. As I neared the hut, my mood lifted slightly, lightened by the abundance of fruits growing right outside the doorpost, which added colors of hope with the offerings of paradise: papaya, pineapple, mango, and the hibiscus flowers we used to brew our morning tea. I could hear their laughter and longings echoing off the water, reminiscing as they continued the conversation from yesterday morning, yesterday afternoon, and last night before bedtime. Their every conversation was filled with graphic descriptions of all the familiar tastes, sights, and sounds of home and life in Southern California. Because they had also lived in Europe and Tokyo, they could recount with clarity all that I'd also been missing. They were giddy with anticipation and anxious to return to urban living. Through these conversations I remained silent, anxious about having to stay on an island, surrounded by overgrown plants and people who'd had enough of the island life.

When I got to the make-shift cabaña, I greeted everyone and took a seat at the table that was covered with freshly picked fruit just arms distance away. I'd been told I could spit the seeds of any fruit directly on the ground and without any nurturing or watering—the only water coming solely from the moisture in the sea air—watch it sprout and shoot up within weeks. I tried to imagine what would grow if I spat out a few guava seeds and burst into tears, the saltwater dripping onto the ground? But I didn't. The others, taking in my welts and swollen eyes, stared at me with shock as I poured a cup of hibiscus tea and helped myself to freshly squeezed pineapple juice and two sea biscuits, or hardtack. If these big bland saltless saltine-type crackers had helped Islanders survive the war, I planned to eat as many as I could in hope of my own survival. A rapid fire of questions: "What happened?" "Are you in pain?" "Whatever happened, why didn't you come get us?"

I smiled weakly, then shared my nightmare with them, "That's not good," they all said. "We can't have you staying in there," Stan said. All of them had grown accustomed to staying in the "native housing" of thatched roofs, using ventilation and island tricks to ward off intruders of every hexapod invertebrates and arthropod phylum, but for some reason, they'd thought I'd be more comfortable in the American-style dormitory.

I agreed to the move out, of course, and quietly sipped my tea and gnawed on my sea biscuits while they exchanged surreptitious glances with each other.

My insect bites interrupted breakfast. Infection was the big concern. Even the slightest cut could become dangerous in the tropics. There was no doctor. No canoes scheduled to come for another week bringing staples. So we applied Tiger Balm to my bites. The salve, made in Singapore and known for its pain relieving and anti-inflammatory qualities, was our cure-all. But it brought no relief. To this day, I carry scars from those water bug-cockroach-looking insects and their bites behind my left ear. Life in paradise makes everything grow bigger. House plants at home are jungle-sized there. Single serving sizes of fruit could be used as a platter to serve a group. The bugs are bigger too. We could have trekked through the jungle to the village on the other side of the island, but after the night before, I didn't want to make the trip, and while the villagers would have known what to do, they most likely would have done what we decided to do—swim in the ocean for the healing effects of the salt water.

I later learned that the language of their silent exchanges at the breakfast table translated as extreme concern about my being on the island too long before the students returned. I was isolated. They wanted to help calm my anxieties, even though they may not have spoken a word or articulated it in a way I could understand. They were sensitive enough people to see me more clearly than I could see myself in that moment. So as an act of distraction and compassion, after swimming, we did what people on island do, we went fishing. Later we grilled the fish we caught, made a variation of fruit salad with seafood, and talked of more swimming and possibly snorkeling later.

When I think about the circumstances I'd endured since arriving in the Solomon Islands—the near rape and abduction, the ugly water bug-cockroaches crawling across and biting my body, it's easy to see the potential for being traumatized to the point of stopping all adventures. When I tell people about my time there, they can't believe I stayed. "Why didn't you just leave?" "I would've been out of there so fast!" But at the time I felt my staying was justified. "You're in paradise," everyone said. This was my dream. It can be easy to justify dysfunction and discomfort when others appear to make it look so normal. However, at some point, I had to learn to distinguish the survival skills specific to me versus the survival skills that worked for others.

Until my near abduction and rape and the giant water bug invasion, I hadn't been aware that I was potentially embracing experiences that could be traumatically or psychologically damaging.

I was encountering my own dragons, fire-breathing circumstances that can scar us in ways not always visible. The way to tame a dragon is to look it straight in the eye. I couldn't do that quite yet. But I couldn't give up. Although the outward signs may diminish, become less visible, some of life's experiences are too vivid, too unforgettable for the inner scars to fade. The details of these experiences not only stay fresh, but with distance between then and now, become clearer. At some point, it helps to have distance in time and place from surreal memories. With distance comes perspective. And while these experiences don't remain front and center, from time to time, they resurface. And when they do, as mine have while writing this chapter, just allow them to linger, to understand the purpose they serve beyond the pain and trauma, and then get on with life. Like dust, I let these memories of the Solomon Islands settle, no longer controlled by the fear of the past, but joyfully hopeful that there is also good around me.

I encourage you to face your dragons. In the quietness of your own thoughts, look around. Find the dark corners where you tuck out of sight your fears and discomforts. Bring them into the light and allow them to be exposed. Give yourself permission to dream of taking new steps, even if they take you in a different direction. Missteps are a part of taking risks.

My hope and prayer for you is that your scars take on new meaning as time passes.

Peace, Be Still

JAMES CLEVELAND

TRUST YOUR INTUITION

*"Why do you go away? So that you can come back.
So that you can see the place you came from
with new eyes and extra colors."*

TERRY PRATCHETT, AUTHOR

My dream of serving in the Peace Corps was rapidly becoming a nightmare, and I wanted to get out it. I wanted off these islands the rest of the world called paradise but to me felt like hell. All of us want to walk within beautiful dreams, not cry through inescapable nightmares. I was no different. I wanted to go to someplace that felt more like heaven to me, like Los Angeles traffic, smog, family, friends, and a more normal chaotic life. But I couldn't allow myself to give up. I'm calm, resilient, shy to the point of pushing the boundaries of my comfort zone to intolerable discomfort, so I handled the situation the only way I knew, the way I'd been handling it since I first set foot in Honiara. I didn't complain, I just dealt with it, telling myself "Just do what you've got to do. Suck it up. Buck up."

After my encounter with the water bug/cockroaches, the

resulting lack of sleep, and my constant dips in the ocean to soothe my swollen itchy skin, I'd been silently chanting my mantra from Deuteronomy 31:6 all day: *"Be strong and courageous. Do not be afraid or terrified because of them, for the Lord your God goes with you; he will never leave you nor forsake you."* Phil, Stan, and Lisa attempted to cheer me up, trying to help me see that I was, in fact, in paradise. I wasn't buying it. They stayed with me all day, and later in the afternoon, after a day of fishing, feasting, and swimming, Phil and Stan suggested I go snorkeling for black coral with them. Lisa planned to stay in the hut. I still can't explain why I switched from my own snorkeling gear and grabbed another mask and snorkel before we set out for the black coral. It was a mistake.

Black coral is rare, most often found in deep waters requiring scuba gear, yet it also grows on the slopes of reefs, and that was the case with the black coral we were looking for. We'd need only snorkeling gear. Because Phil had been injured in the Vietnam War and didn't have the physical capacity to swim in the open ocean with its dangerous undercurrents, we went searching for black coral far up in the channel, miles away from the undercurrent that pulls divers into the open ocean. We walked out quite a way in the shallow waters before we came to a drop-off into deeper waters where the black coral grew along the slope.

We dove under, marveling at the seascape that makes the Solomon Islands a part of the Coral Triangle. It's a hidden world filled with treasures of purple sea plants and fluorescent algae. Clownfish sightings are the norm and with that comes the chance to appreciate the beauty of the flowerlike sea anemone, and its symbiotic bond with the clownfish passing through its bright yellow and green featherlike bushes. Life underwater is a world of its own, and I was drawn to exploring it. The sound of moving water and the sound of your breath synchronize, the power of this is unlike any experience I have had on land. And then there's the visual power and beauty of another world below the surface. I was trying to take in this other realm, to get lost in the experience, but the mask I'd chosen didn't fit properly and kept filling up with water, which affected my ability to breathe properly. I signaled that I was going to go back and change my mask, then started the swim toward shore. But on the way to the shallows, a riptide yanked me under. It was like being caught in the toilet bowl after someone had flushed, the water swirling down, down, as I fought to get to the surface. It all felt slow motion, but it was actually happening in real time faster than my senses could comprehend, dragging me under and out to sea.

Just as we can hear our own heartbeat although it's not audible to others, that's how I heard my breath, uneven and loud, as I struggled to catch it while under water. I listened to the water around me, the deep blue waters taking on a different meaning. My world shrank to the sound of life in my lungs, a physical pull to align with the more peaceful rhythm of my heart breathing. Then I was pulled under again. This cycle continued for what felt like a while—I was up, then sucked under again. Up, sucked under. And finally, I was just up. I tried to get my bearings. I was out in open waters, barely able to make out the shore. So far away. And I was exhausted. So exhausted.

At some point, I no longer saw the coral, but found myself caught in a world between the translucent colors of the water and my own translucent thoughts, images of life passing before me, everything in clear, focused detail — the delicate pattern of my mom's favorite china cup and saucer that she sipped her coffee from every morning; the blue, red, and gray woven threads of my dad's bathrobe (that hangs in my closet right now); the lines across my parents' foreheads when they sat at the dining room table to prepare taxes, pay bills, and read the newspaper. I saw my mom's stationery on which she wrote letters and cards to me and others, saw the pen she wrote with. I saw my sisters, my brother. I saw all these random moments from different stages of my life before me, in black and white, like a 1930s silent picture show.

The sounds of drowning are complex: my lungs fighting for air against the pounding sounds of the current, my voice calling out for help each time I surfaced, my crying out to God internally: "Help me! Please! Help me! Please don't send my body back to them without your breath and life." It would be so sad for my family to receive a body back, my body. No life. No breath. I'd only experienced one death, my grandfather's when I was in third grade. My father had been so sad, the heaviness of his grief having drained the bounce in his step. All the tears. I couldn't let my dad or my family go through that again. My dream from the late '60s to be in the Peace Corps didn't include my life ending as a volunteer in 1978.

What turned me toward faith or what called me to cry out to God was not wanting to see someone else sad. When you know you're loved, you know there's a responsibility that can come with love. I struggled for life with the hope of my family not having to struggle to recover their lives if I died. I struggled for air, to hear the sound of my breath in a different rhythm, at a different volume—regulated, less intense than what I was experiencing in that moment.

And then I believe it was a Greater Love that fed my soul. I was kicking, rising above the surface and being ripped back under with nothing to hold onto other than the snorkel mask that trapped my salty tears and the saltwater surrounding me. Scripture came to mind, the words of God's love, images of people I loved—all affirmed life and gave me strength to keep going.

Another image appeared that I can best describe as a white-gloved hand, like a magician's or mortician's hand, extending toward me. I caught myself reaching for it, inexplicably pulled, as the white-gloved index finger beckoned, seeming to invite me to a restful place, a peaceful place. So peaceful, a lull, a sense of *Come on, just relax, just relax. Don't fight it. Just follow me, come with me.*

You know how you're driving home from a late night out, struggling to keep your eyes open because you're so sleepy? And you start thinking *I'm almost there* and *I'm just going to put my keys on the table and get out of these shoes* and *I'm going to lay my head on the pillow and pull this blanket up around me. I'm going to close my eyes.* And you realize that *Wait!!* You're not in your bed, you're still driving. *Wake up!*

That's what it was like with the hand. I needed to stay in the reality of the moment rather than indulge the comfort of the longing. The part of me that was strong won out. It was if I woke up in that instant, thinking, *Oh no! No! I can't go with you!* It's easy to recognize death when fighting for life. I didn't know that I was still strong enough to fight. I only knew that grabbing onto that gloved hand would lead me in the wrong direction. My last thought was, *I'm not going with you.* It was an out-of-body experience as I watched myself being pulled ashore, and then as I was being resuscitated on shore.

Later, I found out what had happened to me.

After gathering black coral for almost an hour and then starting for shore, Phil and Stan had swum in and were walking back on that long shallow part of the watercourse. Stan must have heard me calling, because he stopped for a moment and turned back to the ocean. "Did you hear that?" he asked Phil.

"Hear what?"

"It sounds like somebody calling out."

But Phil hadn't heard anything.

Then, while Stan was taking in the panoramic view of the open horizon and the mouth of the channel, he thought he spotted something in the water. "What is that out there?" he asked.

But Phil hadn't seen anything.

"I'm going to go and see what that is," Stan said.

Then, expressing what they'd both been thinking, Phil said confidently, "It's been an hour. Gael-Sylvia would have made it back to the hut by now and started back out." They knew I was a strong swimmer, in great shape, and would have made good time.

Stan agreed, figuring since they hadn't run into me, I must have decided to stay in with Lisa since it was getting close to dinner time. But he was pulled to whatever he'd heard and seen in the deeper waters. "I'm going to go see what that is," he said. Then he swam out.

Remember, I was out so far that the last time I had surfaced, the shore had been only a speck, almost blending with the horizon. Stan, the only one strong enough to swim in the fatal undercurrents, the only one who'd heard and seen me, determinedly swam toward me, as what he thought he saw kept appearing and disappearing, shooting to the surface only to be grabbed from below and dragged back under. Stan kept swimming in my direction despite the pressures to return and the oddity of the circumstances. As he drew closer, he saw my hair floating on the water. Then I disappeared suddenly, sucked under again. That water was strong. It was rapid. Then I reappeared, my head barely reaching the surface. I was unconscious but still kicking. Stan grabbed me, struggling fiercely to keep me within his grip, to get us both back to shore alive.

When he got me to the shore outside his hut and was resuscitating me, two boys approached. Nigel and Miguel, two young boys from one of the neighboring Nggela Islands, had quite unexpectedly made the two-hour canoe trip to Siota, which was unusual, especially late in the day, since traveling at night brought the risk of getting lost in the maze of waterways. They'd undertaken the long journey to honor the request of a young lady named Marcianna. Marcianna and I had only met briefly when I was transitioning to live from one island to the next. She understood both places better than I did. She'd been worried about me but couldn't explain why, other than to say she sensed that something was wrong, and she wanted these two kids to go check on me in Siota. She directed them to where they'd find me, and they launched their canoe to navigate through the intricate channels.

It was a two-hour round trip, and they needed to get back before dark. There are more than nine hundred smaller islands among the six major Solomon Islands, creating a massive maze of channels, which makes navigation challenging. A wrong turn and you can end up way off course, stuck in a maze as expansive as the sea. In the intricate maze of waterways, the mountains of the region serve as navigation points. Like everything else that grows naturally in the Solomon Islands, the mountains are extraordinary to behold, their peaks towering above the complex network of channels. Nigel and Miguel wove through the channels, stayed the course, and arrived in two hours from the time they took off. The timing of their arrival — as I was being resuscitated — was nothing short of divine intervention.

Once resuscitated, Lisa gave me a cup of tea to sip, then Stan and Phil wrapped me in cloth to warm me up. They were explaining to me that I needed to get in the canoe with the kids because there was a hospital on their island. Stan, Phil, and Lisa were quite puzzled by the timing of the boys' arrival and how they knew someone was in need and to ask for me specifically. I heard the boys say, in pidgin, "Marcianna, a friend sent us. She said a man name Jesus said for us to go. His spirit was speaking to her spirit and said, 'Go!'" The boys were matter-of-fact about how they came to be here, accepting it as nothing unusual. But Stan, Phil, and Lisa were confused. How could this be? Nevertheless, they loaded my weakened body into the canoe and sent us on our way with the hope that we would make it to shore before sunset.

As the boys paddled, I floated in and out of sleep. I wanted to tell them how thankful I was for their help but because of my limited pidgin and their unfamiliar dialect, it was hard to communicate beyond a smile and a nod of the head. They also patted my feet with a reassurance that I would be okay. There are universal sounds common to all languages, the sounds of laughter, joy, tears, and fears. I understood. But the sun was setting quickly, and the boys had to reach a certain point to avoid veering off course. I heard them talk softly to each other and they sounded worried, fearful.

I asked them what was wrong, and their eyes revealed that they didn't know which channel to go down because it was now dark, and they were worried about making a wrong turn and getting lost in the maze of waterways between the islands. I prayed. Nothing long or elaborate. This was not the time or circumstance. As I write this now, a funny meme comes to mind of a woman from Oklahoma, Kimberly "Sweet Brown" Wilkins, saying, "Ain't nobody got time fo dat!" She had *that* right. There was no energy or time for fear. I prayed out loud from my heart to God's ears, short and to the point: "Lord, light the way and show them the direction they need to go. Lord, you can light the way." And I kid you not, within a matter of a few seconds, at the most a few minutes, it was as if the sun rose again briefly, as if there was a shower of shooting stars, the illumination sufficient to light our way.

Nigel and Miguel didn't touch me after that. They scooted away, in fact, looking at me and then each other as though wanting to say, "Don't touch her! Who is dat!?" Before falling asleep again, I remember saying, "Oh, thank you, Jesus," and then I was out. This light show occurred two more times before we reached our destination, showing us the way to go. The boys whispered to one another and later to the people waiting at the dock, including Marcianna, who sat in the night air anticipating our safe arrival. "She like torch belong Jesus. Torch belong Jesus." That was their pidgin reference to the missionaries who'd been a part of the islands' buried history, carrying flashlights as torches and their Book filled with miracles.

A public award was presented to Stan for saving my life. It was the talk of the island and a headline story in the local newspaper. When I left, my near drowning was the reason I gave for leaving the island prematurely. Although I'd survived the near drowning in the ocean, privately, internally, it was more complicated. While I knew I needed to leave—how many more signs did I need?— I felt that I'd failed and was leaving prematurely, running back home and leaving "paradise" and all the people who'd welcomed me, depended on me. I felt like I would let them down by running back home. The night before I left, I was lying on my bed in the Peace Corps Director's guest bedroom, staring at the ceiling fan, swatting mosquitos, tears streaming down my face, feeling confused and sad that a dream come true wouldn't end on a happy note. Then I thought of Switzerland, Shirley Temple, and a conversation from the film Heidi, when Fräulein Rottenmeier accuses Heidi of running away, and Heidi says, "I wasn't running away! I was just going home by myself!"

Those words brought me such peace. From that moment on, I embraced the word of God even more than I had before. When I got home, I chose quotes from scripture, favorite books, a line I found in an article to remind me of profound life lessons. I kept these lines where I could refer to them. This would serve me well in my life, during the times I felt like I was going under, lost, or uncertain if I was being heard on Earth and in Heaven. And also during those moments of deep despair, times when we cannot do anything by our own strength, times that require something greater within us. It's a continuing battle of trying to figure out what can I do within my own strength and where I rely on His strength. Having experienced the miraculous, I now know it's reasonable to expect nothing less.

To experience the power of God's loving, we don't always have to be in a crisis state. We can experience God within the ordinary routines of life. While folding laundry, we can thank God for the healthy bodies that wear the clothes fresh from the dryer. While driving, we can give thanks for keeping us safe on the road, and after reaching our destination, for arriving safely. We can give thanks for a moment of quiet amid the sounds arising from the hustle and bustle around us. These moments and more can be filled with gratitude, which opens us to giving help to and receiving help from others, and a deeper knowing of what we need to truly feel safe and at home.

I would like to encourage you to keep fighting for life. Call for help. Kick and cry out if you must. Know that He has you in His grip and that someone will hear you and respond. New life can be breathed into the most desperate circumstances. Sometimes the search for the rarest of treasures is knowing that there are others who hear what no one else can hear, see what no one else can see. It's never too late for them to show up, as long as you don't give up.

I hope and pray that you marvel at the world and all you encounter each day. In each moment note marvelous details that make life richer. You don't have to feel that you're running away from everything in life. You're just trying to steer your canoe in the right direction. And by the light of God and the love He places within the hearts of others, you will arrive, be resuscitated, and find a place you can call home.

PART II

REIGNITING A SENSE OF *joy*

Every day, we're provided with a gift of beauty that we can be thankful for. This beauty surrounds us to cheer us and help us reach places of joy and contentment. It may come as a burst of colorful flowers, the bright blue sky, or fresh snow blanketing the trees on a winter morning. It may come through the smile of a child, stranger, employer, receptionist, co-worker, or the sound of a foreign voice from a call center or a loved one on the other side of the world. It may come through a song, a picture, a favorite quotation, a quiet moment, or seeing an opportunity and taking a chance. God has provided a special gift to remind us of the details in life that are sources of joy. We begin here to see anew and to reignite what we knew as children—a sense of joy.

Song OF THE DAY

Every Praise
HEZEKIAH WALKER

THE SIMPLICITY OF PRAYER

"Nature is the one song of praise that never stops singing."

RICHARD ROHR

The leap of faith to trust in something greater is an act of gratitude and it begins with the simplicity of prayer. Prayer innately carries power. Connecting with the energy and practice of prayer, communing with God, is an effective practice of making deposits into our soul's account. Prayer is how I acknowledge that there's someone greater than me who can do great things in ways that I can't. When I experience the power of simple prayers and the magnitude of great prayers answered, I can't help but be thankful, often breaking out into songs of gratitude. This is worship. This is the truth of why and how prayer and gratitude can't help but co-exist in my heart.

This is why it's become a daily desire for me to pray throughout the day, especially for others. I pray for my employees, the mailman, the neighbor, the city council members, the White House staff and their families, the clerk at the gas station, the truck driver on the freeway—everyone, everywhere, anytime. Life is so much more than what our eyes can see. I can't claim to know everything within this magnificent universe. So I ask. Being of completely sound mind and open heart, I talk to God and then listen. I ask the Grand Creator of All Life to speak into my thoughts what only He can fully understand, the details of what He alone can know and then make it clear to me how I am to respond.

I ask God how I should pray for others, to reveal through the Holy Spirit an understanding that can only come from an Infinite Being into my finite mind. Sometimes I pray for their fears, their families, their hopes, their health, the whole of who they are, regardless of their roles, influence and status. It's a random act of kindness with long-lasting impact. I'm praying for Kelly, my book coach and editor, as I write these words. I pray for her to have a clear mind, sharp focus, and the understanding to fully capture the unwritten parts of the message conveyed within these written words. I pray like this for everyone. Throughout the day, I am in prayer. Keep in mind, I'm not walking around tossing out crazy words at random strangers or wearing a sign around my neck that reads, "I'm praying for you!" My prayers are private thoughts that periodically have miracle moments presented as opportunities to connect with others in very unexpected ways.

Here's one example. In the mid-months of 2011, an economic tsunami was heading toward our newly-planted life in Tucson, Arizona, and our financially volatile business at the border of Mexico and the United States. It was heading right for us, about to rip at all we'd built, like I'd seen on CNN broadcasts of hurricanes tearing roofs off homes, casting them miles away from their original foundations. We'd not only uprooted our lives to move from another state, but those of employees who trusted our leadership. We had the stability of investments in our homes and important relationships and the excitement of the prospect of expanding life for all of us.

We'd left behind personal, political, and community relationships, along with our McDonald's franchise business in Ohio, which included numerous restaurants, real estate investments associated with employee housing, employee-related commitments, and other business and personal ventures. Our new venture included building McDonald's restaurants and a proposed La Quinta hotel in a place that would get us much closer to home in Southern California: Arizona, near the United States-Mexico border.

But two years later our business investments were going south, a combination of The Great Recession having hit hardest in the Southwest and the crime at our section of the United States-Mexico border having taken an epic upturn as drug lords between the two neighboring border states of Arizona and Sonora infused the environment with bloody tragedies, restricting my ability to live near and work in Mexico just as it was doing to our employees and customers.

Ambos Nogales, or both Nogales, is how life at the border is represented in the two border cities of Nogales, Arizona, US, and Nogales, Sonora, Mexico. Life continues with a natural ebb and flow and no visible barriers. The two are as one, although different. We settled into our home in the Tucson area, about an hour and a half north, while running our business and relationships within Ambos Nogales. As naturally as produce is transported by trucks coming and going across the border, children, employees, and our family crossed the border, blending life in two countries that are connected as one. Our visibility was known on billboards and broadcasts, in schools and community engagements, at weddings and birthdays, and so much more. We were active participants in life in both worlds, and we loved the people.

But with the drug wars, tensions were high. How could we have become the characters in a real-life scenario most often seen as "entertainment drama" on the big screens or news? Yet it was happening, and it wasn't fiction. The previous two years we'd hosted a bi-national community celebration attracting thousands. That year, the mayor of Nogales had called to advise me and our family not to cross the border for fear of a potential kidnapping and also to postpone a high-profile community event of serving McDonald's meals, providing school supplies, and celebrating life as a community without barriers—because of intel his office had received of violence being planned. Life as we'd come to know it came to a halt with this unexpected new crisis.

Within the first two years of our arrival, a once serene border community and tourist destination had become the center of a war between two-rival drug cartels, including ambushes, murders, and the loss of lives close to many of us. In the privacy of our own fears, associated with so many unexpected losses, we were in need of a form of life support that was beyond the comprehension of most, including ourselves. We began to see our dreams among the casualties that were beyond our ability to control. It was devasting.

All of us, our bankers, employees, community, and business partners, needed our lives and our profit and loss (P&L) statements to once again balance. The pressures of living, mourning, doing business, and meeting church/social/philanthropic obligations that were once manageable pulled at me. Life was a tangled mess and it was beginning to unravel. The complexity of building restaurants and a proposed hotel, along with new relationships in a new cultural, political, and economic environment made it difficult to see clear pathways and new directions. Without exaggeration, our everyday decisions included matters of life and death. It was a heavy burden that weighed on us every hour of every day.

My husband was stressed, and my heart felt like it was breaking. Have you ever found yourself reaching for a favorite piece of jewelry that you'd thoughtlessly tossed among a mess of intertwined necklaces? Or tried to detangle matted hair when you were in a hurry? Or pulled the wrong loose thread and partially unraveled the entire hem? Each attempt saws on your fraying nerves. Getting our lives back to normal was like that. Getting our business back to normal was like that. And then my father had a massive stroke, during an otherwise relaxing day. I flew to Southern California immediately. I needed God to make things normal again, to make them right.

We managed a strong outward show of calm to disguise the inner turmoil that only our accountant and corporate partners understood. The insanity was taking a toll on our health and the price was high. During a crisis, we all still have the ability to make choices. Mark and I chose to stay grounded in our faith, our marriage, and our commitment to our employees as best we could, and to our ethics.

Each week we juggled meeting payroll, while one restaurant was closed during the construction of another. We needed a sign to let us know that all would be well, a glimpse of a happy ending, or just a hint of what to do. Could we ride it out or were we going to get slammed and have to pull the plug? The changing health care laws and the glaring possibility of letting employees go added to the tangled mess of our lives. Cutting out the knot as you would a piece of gum at the center of a tangled knot of hair wasn't the best answer. We weren't willing to cut people's livelihoods.

Past commitments made during peaceful times pulled at us from one end, while present circumstances tried to drag us down. In this unstable place, I'd completely forgotten that I was scheduled to travel to Belize to explore a partnership with the First Lady, Kim Simpliss Barrow, through a philanthropic project. Our family's recent public philanthropic commitment required a strategic plan, a partner with a global track record, integrity, and a compatible heart to acknowledge leadership not often associated with nations of color, including Mexico.

I'd been in the hospital for seven straight days, sleeping curled near my father's bed on two chairs pushed together, wearing the same dress. My hair was a mess. My life was a mess. And then a reminder appeared on my phone as unexpectedly as the text I'd received notifying me that my Dad had been rushed to the hospital for a stroke just a few days before. The invitation to explore possibilities associated with the First Lady of Belize came by way of introductions through Project C.U.R.E. (Commission on Urgent Relief and Equipment), whose mission is to identify, solicit, collect, sort, and distribute medical supplies and services according to the needs of the world. The Belize reminder appeared via email in the form of boarding pass for a Delta flight out of Tucson, one state away from where I was at the moment. I'd forgotten all about it during the months that had passed since my commitment. The boarding pass notification for a "dream trip" no longer held the appeal it once had.

"Oh, yes! That's right!" I told my husband and son on the phone the night after receiving the boarding pass. "I'm supposed to travel to Belize with the CEO of Project C.U.R.E. to witness first-hand the impactful work they do with the First Lady of Belize. But I'm not going." The thought of my father passing away and my husband, fatigued and alone, dealing with our personal life-threatening circumstances while I went to a place most people associate with vacation and fun—*No way!* They both responded with pretty much the same words: "I think you're supposed to go. I think the Lord wants you to go because it's about something bigger and you have the heart to see and act on it. All of us will be fine. But you do need to go." The email had arrived just as the triage nurse assured me that, after seven days of intensive care, my father was comfortably resting. Less than twenty-four hours later, I was in Belize.

Although I don't remember traveling from the hospital in California back to Arizona, I do remember the impact the Belize trip had on me. My husband had packed fresh clothes, gassed my car for my two-hour drive to the Phoenix Airport, and had my office assistant assemble all my notes. It reaffirmed my approach to philanthropy and my commitment to trust my response to the needs all of us see. Others cared about me and my desires apart from my day-to-day roles. Others wanted to see me succeed and these kind acts were one of the many ways loving support was provided.

After my years researching money management that included generational philanthropic legacies, this trip had been a prayer come true. But now, this answered prayer seemed poorly timed. Life had other priorities and going to Belize was the last thing on my mind. I was exhausted, and if I missed the flight from Phoenix, no problem. I couldn't think rationally. I just wanted to sleep. If I missed the flight, I'd stay awake long enough to either check into a hotel, pull into a roadside parking lot, or make the two-hour trip back home to climb into our bed—any of these choices would be respite after days of sleeping in my makeshift two-chair bed.

I made it to the airport just in time, but I was delayed due to airport construction. Although I'd flown out of Tucson International Airport with enough regularity that the skycaps recognized my car and knew me by name, I hadn't booked this trip, so I was flying on a different airline located in another terminal, which I was unfamiliar with. Usually, navigating airport construction and circling hard to reach terminals could be a bit frustrating, but I was too tired to care. To make my flight I needed (1) a miracle or (2) a miracle. I was too exhausted to feel worried and my stress level was already at an all-time high, so the only option was to pray: "Lord, if you want me on this plane and in Belize you'll need to send an angel."

As I drove up to the unfamiliar terminal, I saw a skycap and slowed down to cross traffic to the curb but stopped when I saw that his line was too long. Another skycap saw me slow down. We made eye contact. Something in my expression must have spoken to him, because with a family of five in front of him, all with pink suitcases, he stepped away and motioned for me to roll down my window. "International or domestic?"

"International," I shouted.

He waved me over to a no parking zone, reached through my passenger window, took my passport and phone (to check my boarding pass), pointed to my convertible red Mercedes, and said, "How much do you like your car?"

I laughed, a weak tired laugh, and said, "I like my car a lot."

"Good. Stay with it." I assumed he didn't want my car to get towed. Then, "How many bags do you have?"

"One," I said, as he grabbed my cheetah print luggage my

husband had lovingly packed from my passenger seat.

I got out of the car, waiting for him to return, hoping the TSA patrol didn't spot me and make me move. When he returned, he handed me my printed boarding passes, while the family of five, with their pink suitcases talked and waited patiently. "You have to get to the gate fast," he said. "They start boarding at 6:40, and it's 6:20."

"Where's the closest parking?" Exhaustion had my normally soft voice at a whisper.

He had me turn around as he pointed to a parking structure entry directly in front of me. "I saved a space just for you," he said. "Now go!"

As I turned back to look him in his eyes, I said, "Let me give you this tip. What's your name? I'm so thankful for you."

He looked me straight in the eye, laughed, and said jokingly, "Don't make the tip too big, because that means I'll have to tithe more." Then he lifted his jacket lapel to reveal a name badge that read, "Jesus."

I laughed. "Jesus?!"

"Yes, my name is Jesus."

I had remained where he had instructed, standing guard near the car. Now I moved closer, hugged him, and said, "Man! God's a trip! I asked for an angel and He sent Jesus! Thank you! Thank you so much!"

Now that could seem like a nice pleasant coincidence, but that's not my point. As I rode the escalator to the second floor for TSA security clearance, I could see the line backed up all the way to the Brighton store. If I were going to make my flight, it would take three more TSA agents showing up and another miracle. The good thing about exhaustion and/or life being out of control, out of *our* control, is that we get out of God's way and He can show up in ways that we would have missed and blocked had we been more alert and under the illusion that we're in control.

So I just stood in the line. If I missed the "dream opportunity" at the other end of this flight, okay. If I made it, well okay, too, as long as I had my window seat and could sleep. People were getting restless, irritable, complaining. The people in front of and behind me attempted to engage me in their complaining. Not interested. Didn't care. I acted invisible and let them ignore me.

My mind wandered all over the globe as I thought about an event I'd recently hosted in Tucson in response to the amazing women and girls around me who didn't realize that their most sacred dreams held value. The event was Girls Fly! and it embodied my life's purpose, a response to all the good around me. I wondered what would happen if women and girls in other countries in Europe, Asia, Scandinavia, and Africa could experience what the 628 attendees at the Girls Fly! event had? Girls Fly! is an empowerment program I founded in 2010 that encourages women and girls from all age groups and all walks of life to pursue a wide range of personal and professional aspirations through fun, inspirational presentations, mentoring, and interactive experiences.

And then, I saw a lady coming up the escalator wearing jeans with sequined pockets and a pink boa-looking scarf, who stopped at the top of the escalator, blocking other stunned ticket holders as all of them stared in disbelief at the growing line. It was the shrinking of her shoulders and the tears filling her eyes that made me pray for her. Her. I was there to pray for her. "Lord, how should I pray for her? *Pray for her not to be discouraged,* I heard these words in my heart: *"Pray that she knows I am near; that her family will make it through the relationship and work challenges; that he will come to see that I love him even more than she does; Pray that she not be discouraged or give up.*" I had no idea who "he" was. I didn't need to know. I just prayed using the words He had given. I also prayed that the woman made her flight, that she had a trip of peace and unexpected renewal. Amen.

Within moments, two TSA agents arrived. Half asleep, half hoping I could go back home, I blindly went through the familiar motions of removing shoes and jewelry and waiting to clear security when I heard the laughing voice of someone say, "Gael-Sylvia, what are you doing flying out of this terminal?!" It was a family friend who normally worked the terminal I usually flew out of, but in all these years, I had never crossed paths with him. We laughed and I asked why he was on this side. His answer, "God assigned it. They needed help and I told my boss to send me where there are probably people needing to get flights, since some are delayed. Hey, you're just on time. You plane is about to close the doors." I looked back but couldn't see the lady with the pink boa, so I whispered the prayer that she would make her flight.

I made the flight. I had my window seat. I curled up as I tried to distinguish the accent from the lady seated behind me. It's a fun game and an ice breaker when meeting new people, to try to pinpoint their accent, but this wasn't the time or place, so I went to sleep.

When I arrived at Philip S.W. Goldson International Airport in Belize City, I was met by a greeting party. Mike—the man responsible for my being there—was the only person I recognized. We'd met once through a philanthropic organization only a couple of months prior. He'd introduced me to Project C.U.R.E and we had discussed our mutual interest of diversifying and increasing accessibility to women who lead nations and increasing visibility to those who are often ignored. My philanthropic focus highlights the various levels of accomplishments among women and girls, especially women and girls of color who are often viewed as being only on the receiving end of philanthropic ventures, when the facts reveal that more often than realized, women and nations of color are also on the giving end. This includes the increased visibility of women who are the first ladies of nations. My motto is "Whether the mother to one or to millions, most often the first person of influence in our lives is a mother, a woman."

I'm also associated with a global group of women philanthropists, Women Moving Millions, whose mission is to catalyze unprecedented resources for the advancement of women and girls. Members include such powerful women as Gloria Steinem, Helen LaKelly Hunt, and Abby Disney. The organization is about documenting the herstory of female philanthropic leadership, influencing the voice of and perspective on how herstory's being shaped for women. My objective is to ensure that these predominately White, well-intended women influencing the chronicling of events capture the whole story by including women philanthropists of color and leaders as well, to advance the visibility of women from our country and nations of color, who are often ignored yet are in-fact influential leaders.

Mike directed me to an awaiting van outside of baggage claim, along with approximately fifteen other guests. Smiling as I passed others already seated, I sat in the only available seat next to a woman named Michelle. We acknowledged each another with a smile and a quick name exchange.

Two days later, on a free day during our packed schedule of long site visits, I decided to stay back at the hotel. When I went down to breakfast, one of the only seats left was next to Michelle from our group. Turned out that both of us were exhausted and, while under different circumstances we would have enjoyed the company of the others, we'd both stayed behind, embracing our solitude. The anticipated alone time turned into mutual support as we got acquainted. Within moments we connected, not because of our reasons for being on this philanthropic travel trip —hers to explore her potential role as donor and board member, and me to explore mine as donor and partner—but about why we chose to stay behind on a free day. I stayed because my life as I knew it to be had recently been riddled with the possibility of my father dying, the instability of the bank world, and shifting finance guidelines, which she could readily understand without my delving deeply into my personal affairs and exhaustion. I told her that I'd prayed for the lady with the sequined jeans and pink boa-style scarf. I shared the exact words God spoke to my heart on behalf of hers.

Michelle, a single mother and investment banker, stayed because of her exhaustion with the shifting financial markets, the shifting dynamic in her cross-country relationship with her fiancé, and the resulting drama that was taking its toll on her decision-making ability. Without having to delve deeply, I also understood what she was saying and what had not yet been spoken. There was more to this woman's story, I was sure, a lot more, because there was more to mine.

I wasn't my normally extroverted, curious, friendly self. I was tired. My mind was tired, my mouth seemed to be at a loss for words, my throat tight from all the tension of talking to nurses, doctors, medical staff about a life that held less value for them than for my family and me. My body needed rest. I needed to be alone to inhale the peaceful surroundings and hope that I could breathe in and hold onto enough of this peace so I could return home in seven days with a clearer mind, encouraging words, and a refreshed perspective.

Yet during the next fifteen hours, the rest of our free day, Michelle and I bonded over meals, horseback riding in the outback, on into the early morning hours in the jacuzzi. There we learned more to one another's life story, a lot more. Our lives would stay closely intertwined as we encouraged and prayed one another through life's challenges over the next two years. Hardly a morning, afternoon, or evening would pass without us talking, texting, or traveling to visit to one another. She and her fiancé are married now, living in the same state, with two miracle children creating a peaceful family. The trip to Belize brought a new friendship and opened doors to bigger miracles. I would return two years later to work with the First Lady of Belize and encourage women and girls through Girls Fly!

I believe one of the greatest acts of kindness and love is when we see someone lost, confused, hurting, bewildered, or angry and join their heart's cry to God. Most people don't live a praying life. Prayer for many is isolated to the private closets of their lives, moments of deep distress, a crisis, or within a designated place of religious worship. For me, every day is a day of worship, because worship comes from a place of gratitude and perspective, the practice of seeing every detail as a gift to be cherished and a reminder that I'm not alone on this journey called life on Earth. I have to make deposits into the invisible parts of who I am, nurture those parts in such a way that my external life reveals the whole of who I am. Without the practice of making these deposits, we have a minimal or negative balance to withdraw from. I can hardly wait to grab my Bible and sit in the quiet of the morning or on a break during the most hectic of days to see what God has to say to me.

Yes! Ask God to speak to you, to help you see and hear how near He is. Ask God to help you understand what a verse means and then live it out in your daily life. And as He does, don't discount the new answers as mere coincidence. Answers might appear in many ways—the power of praying as a random act of kindness that can lead to new friendships and worlds of opportunities at every level of life as Girls Fly! has done, having Jesus show up as an angel dressed as a skycap, your children encouraging you to keep going, having your husband fill your car with gas when you're pressed for time. The more you see and experience the truth of this, of a Living God, the more you'll want to experience it. This is why joy can be refreshed during the most challenging moments of life, and you can live more clearly, with fresh eyes and ears, secure in the knowledge that you're not alone.

When you choose daily to be intentional in looking for fresh perspectives to give and receive random acts of kindness, you can experience the power of prayer, the power of scripture. You can access images, songs, and quotations to engage that power in your entire being—your heart, mind, and spirit. It's well documented that this is a common spiritual practice across many faiths. My point of reference is the Bible and you, too, may be surprised at the insights you will gain by exploring it. For example, I have "A Verse of the Day," a daily Bible verse that's the theme for how I will consciously choose to think about life, to see the presence of God, and to help guide my words, thoughts, and actions throughout each day. I select this verse at the start of every new day. Without this practice, I feel like I'm wondering mindlessly and aimlessly. My purpose and the value of my actions feels minimal. But when I look at each moment, each opportunity, each person, and each circumstance through the words of God, I sense a deeper value mixed within the grandest of dreams and the smallest of deeds.

I encourage you to be open to others. Be open to exploring new places near and far. You'll discover the possibility of new friendships from the most unexpected places. If you're holding onto the hope of doing something bigger, and you're doubting the value of believing in yourself, your dream, God, or your own less-than-ideal circumstances.

It's my hope and prayer that you will feel encouraged to hold on. Stay strong. Believe.

"I think you're supposed to go. I think the Lord wants you to go because it's possibly about something bigger and small steps can land you there without you being fully aware of how it all happened. All of us will be fine."

Song OF THE DAY

Roar

KATY PERRY

LEADING WITH GRATITUDE

"Some walks you have to take alone."

MOCKINGJAY, SUZANNE COLLINS

"There are moments in life when you have to be willing to walk alone. Many who started with you won't finish with you."

GAEL-SYLVIA PULLEN

I start each day with a prayer of gratitude, acknowledging the finest details of what I'm thankful for. Then I select one item, open my eyes, write it down in my gratitude journal, and make that top of mind all day. I also have a more consistent practice of bookending my days with Gratitude Walks, one in the morning or early afternoon and then one at night. This helps me calibrate my mental and emotional priorities, to be mindful in my actions and priorities, to align with purpose to my task of the day. It's a habit of awareness and intentional choices to align with the Spirit of God and what I believe I'm called on to contribute in life each day. It's a way of laying brick after brick on a proverbial yellow brick road to places of awe, wonder, and service to others.

I generally tie these walks to walking the dog. It's great that we have a dog because otherwise there would be times when I wouldn't necessarily feel like going and probably wouldn't. But dogs are in charge, so I go. My morning walks are a way to thank God for the new day, and to think about not only what I have to do that day, but to also feed my soul. I often listen to worship songs as I walk, or thought-provoking, inspirational podcasts for all areas of interest, from home décor to business, sermons to self-help, health to autobiography. Or sometimes I just walk in the morning quiet. These walks have been a part of my day for as long as I can remember.

During my evening walks, my perspective is slightly different. I'm giving gratitude, in the still darkness of night, I give gratitude for the day that's ending, and for the light God continues to provide, even in the dark, the moon and the stars and the shadows they cast, the silhouettes they create. I spend this time just being thankful. Now this is not to say that there aren't moments when I'm just absolutely ticked off at somebody or something, and fuming, walking it off; those moments do happen. But I find that my ticked-off state doesn't last as long and I'm able to get back to a place of calm a lot quicker than if I were inside.

Committing to the practice, and being disciplined about the practice, focusing on what you have to be grateful for, shortens the time needed for reflection on an upsetting issue, being lost in the power of a negative moment, or staying in the negative loop. And that frees up time and energy to put into the positives, put into the life-producing and the energy-producing.

It's true. This quiet time of gratitude gives us the strength to recognize the distinguishable voice of God. Being guided by the voice of God and not the chatter of our own self-talk gives us the courage and confident assurance to do essential things, such as knowing when we've wronged another person, and when we need to take responsibility for what we've done, admit being wrong, and apologize. There's a strength that comes from taking ownership and setting things right.

Most of us could easily justify feeling frustrated if our car broke down along a highway during intense summer heat, with two children in diapers and car seats, while rushing to the post office before closing to ensure a deadline is met. That happened to me four summers ago, but instead of reacting with frustration, I told the children to pray that the Lord would send an angel as I phoned for roadside service from AAA. Not long after their prayer, they saw a tow truck pulling up to us, thirty minutes earlier than estimated. They screamed with joyful excitement, yelling "Look! Look! The angel is here. Aren't we glad we can talk to God and He hears us and cares?" They wanted to meet the angel. I told him the story and he was touched. As he peeked his head into the air-conditioned car, he smiled and said, "Hey, kids. How did you know I needed someone to pray for me today? I was having a rough morning in all this heat and I was hoping the afternoon customers would appreciate all that it takes to do what I do. Thank you." Our angel turned out to be extremely kind and helpful.

Not long ago, almost four years to the day and near the same location, my tire blew out. I prayed differently this time: "God, I remember your kindness toward me and may whoever is coming to assist me today know that I'm praying for them too." The same tow truck driver showed up! Yes! Four years later. It was his last day on a job he had been doing for twenty-one years. I asked him if he remembered me and those two children. His response, "Not only have I remembered that day, but the gratitude all of you expressed toward me changed the way I looked at my own life and this job. I'm calmer, more appreciative of the small things, and able to close out the last few hours of this job with joy and happiness. I thank you for that." Joy and happiness. For others and for me, I welcome joy and happiness as outcomes from life's random inconveniences.

I don't want "being upset" to be the habit or personality or behavior associated with me. But don't get it twisted. I will end up in fights about issues I believe in firmly, and I will not tolerate injustice, even if it's rudeness toward me or towards someone else. My gratitude practices help me determine where I'm going to focus my energy, what I'm going to fight for, whether I need to fight, and then if I'm wrong, what I need to do to make things right There have been times where I've recognized the need to apologize immediately and gone back to the cashier in the grocery store or the salesperson or the postal clerk, and said, "You know what? I just need to apologize to you because I was pretty rude, and you didn't deserve that. I just wanted to tell you I'm sorry."

There have been times when I've been driving away and I've heard the Lord's words: "Seriously, Gael-Sylvia, you just better go back." My initial reactions are always excuses like "Oh man! I'm going to be late for my appointment" or "If she hadn't done this, then I wouldn't have done that." But I have to take responsibility for the parts I'm responsible for, so I turn around and go back, or I'll go back later, or I'll go get a card and I'll go back and drop it off, leave it with the manager.

I want a compliment to be as easy as when I've had to call the manager and say, "You've got a person over here that's not very good." Everything isn't complicated. I don't get this right every time. I don't respond as quickly as I'd like. I say a prayer about being better able to share, to respond quicker and express an appreciation for the good that is around me that allows me to live, breathe, and act from a place of joy.

Gratitude is defined as the quality of being thankful, having a readiness to show appreciation for and to return kindness. Deep gratitude has to come from within and in a meaningful way. To find it we have to also embrace quiet, which is the peace that comes from bookending our days by acknowledging the good around us.

I encourage you to see how different life feels when you take a gratitude walk in the morning, naming all that you are thankful for as you anticipate the new day, as you pour out your worries, breathe, observe, and walk. Try it without anyone else and at first without music. Let the sound of your own breath, your own footsteps, and the sound of your own thoughts keep you company. You'll feel refreshed. I encourage you to do the same at night. The sounds of darkness are often the most beautiful because they're the most unfamiliar.

I hope and pray that the darkness of evening also sheds light on how you perceive the unknown. You will be surprised by how much you've been missing, especially when you get a glimpse of a shooting star.

Songs OF THE DAY

Don't Play that Song
ARETHA FRANKLIN

A FEW OF THE SONGS MY GRANDMOTHER SANG...

Lord Keep Me Day by Day
ALBERTINA WALKER

You Can't Beat God Giving
BILLY PRESTON

I Love the Lord
JENNIFER HOLLIDAY, DONALD VAILS

THE POWER OF A SONG

*"People who are crazy enough to think they can
change the world, are the ones who do."*

ROB SILTANEN

Have you ever been curious about how a song, smell, image, or taste can instantly transport you from the present moment to a long-forgotten experience? I continue to hold the belief that if I want happy memories later, then now is the time to create them. Singing and music are an important of the future memories being established right now. So in addition to my practice of selecting a verse from scripture for the day, I also select a Song of the Day.

Incorporating a theme song into your day is powerful. I grew up with a paternal grandmother who was always humming a tune. Most often them were hymns and Negro spirituals or gospel. Always something new. I used to wonder how she could know so many. Cleaning chicken, whipping cake batter, folding laundry—I learned the rhythms of life based on the tunes coming from her lips. Music filled our home. We were not musicians, but music filled our household. The songs she sang into our hearts are precious heirlooms, memories, like seeds, pressed deep into the soil of our childhood, providing my brother, sisters, and me with a reminder and confidence that all is well, or the expectation that it would be.

Hearing melodies without words is like breathing in the inviting smells coming from the oven before seeing the food. Each communicates a message that strengthens the bond that tethers one generation to the next. The sound of my grandmother humming a song as she rolled out the sticky biscuit dough on floured cutting boards or coated chicken to fry seemed to make everything taste better. It appeared that the songs in her head made her wash dishes and clean both hers and other people's homes as if it were sacred work. The fruits of her love are a lingering sweet taste that have carried us through the sourest of times. I've intentionally created (and continue to create) moments to pass on to the next generation, which now includes our own grandchildren, grand nieces, and nephews. And now that we're living at the beach, the sweet atmosphere filled with the tang of salt air adds to the memories we create together with songs, peace, and laughter.

I may not fry chicken or have a routine of making biscuits, but music fills our home just the same and a Song of the Day fills the spaces within my thoughts. Songs create images that help carry me forward, no matter what I'm going through. The power of the image helps to shape my thinking and my own internal thoughts and perspectives through the day. And it helps me to be more patient. To be more joyful, more peaceful. And sometimes when the images fade or the song is blasted out of my head because of whatever I'm dealing with, I just internally get quiet and reflect back to the scripture and the prayer from earlier in the morning, which centers me, opening the space to let the song back in.

Regardless of my circumstances, there's a tune deep within my soul that I draw upon the way women draw water from wells. Research shows that our mental state has measurable physical influence on us, more specifically, on our DNA. I want my soul to sing, and I want to ensure ultimate maximum impact upon my DNA. That's why I sing. That's why I love music. Singing is my thermostat changing my mood. It's how I preset the temperature of my temperament. This means, music helps me choose my mindset, the mood I'm in or want to move toward. It speaks for me when I have no words of my own. It helps me course-correct almost as efficiently as my computer's autocorrect, but with more accuracy.

Music and singing aid my decision-making when advice doesn't come from others. It provides wisdom and insight when I'm blind to my own inability to make right decisions. It raises up emotions, feelings in me that have been lingering just below the surface, until just the right note and perfectly-timed melody push them to the frontline of my thoughts, like an athlete tired of sitting on the sideline and forcing his or her way into the game of my life.

Bob Marley may have believed that "One good thing about music, when it hits you, you feel no pain," but music can also hit hard. While music evokes our fondest memories, our laughter and highest aspirations, it also can evoke our fears, grief, and pain. I'm a big fan of the Rollin' Stones, and I've been known to have Keith Richard's guitar riffs on auto replay for hours, not speaking in particular words but speaking in emotions, down to the marrow in the bones. It's in the bones.

As a child, I watched my older brother jimmy-rig a record player arm with a pencil and rubber band to replay a single part of a song over and over again until the needle created a groove and the record was ruined. Years, later, inspired by my brother's inventiveness, I would take cassette tapes and record the same parts of a song or my favorite single back to back on both sides, bringing 90–120 minutes of "instant replays" to my portable players. We never had a reel-to-reel, but I wished for one. That way, I could reel-to-reel more than eight hours of a favorite tune. And now, by selecting a Song of the Day, I can play that music inside, hum along. It's on a twenty-four-hour loop.

Music gets deep within the crevices of my soul's memories, feeds my thoughts, causes my imagination to soar, and gives life to everything around me. Like life, a cluster of notes or sequence of chords can be repeated over and over again, or it may be heard only once, as with, say, a lead guitar solo. There are moments in life that are riffs. They can be minor decorative elements or they can be the basis of a life song. Such is life. Such is the essential power of expressing gratitude and memorializing it in a Song of the Day. It's a way of acknowledging the good around us and saying "thank you" to God for repeatedly showing up and providing guidance, balance, and joy.

Each of my *Songs of the Day* is an expression of words I lack to string together on my own, set to music with a rhythm and cadence and a mix of sounds, notes too high for me to reach with my vocal cords but low enough to be within reach of my heart. Among the various tones and voices are lyrics in various languages. I understand all of them even when I don't know a word they're saying. My heart translates the meaning into experiences within my own life. Even the resting points between each note have a shared place of value within all the movement. In these moments of rest, I experience what scientists have confirmed: the brain releases dopamine, and that natural anti-depressant, in times of deep despair, can be addictive, creating an internal environment of comfort, confidence, and movement through the unconscious parts of life with intentional rhythm. Singing is my compass. It's the superfood my brain thrives on to stimulate my creativity. Music does to my soul what verses and quotes do for my brain — it ensures that I live and lead from a place of joy, even in the joyless moments.

I encourage you to play music today that captures your feelings. Hopefully, it will make you smile or encourage you throughout your day. The only consideration is to avoid including songs that feed your fury and drive you in a direction opposite of hope and joy. Let the song play on repeat. Walk with it. Work with it. Cook or eat to it. Smile because of it. Try it again the next day. Or pick a new song.

It's my hope and prayer for you that today will be the start of a new you. It's a new day. A new song. A new memory. Filling your day with a song infuses your memories with the same uplifting feeling, the same joy and hope.

Song OF THE DAY

Vivir Mi Vida
MARC ANTHONY

THE POWER OF A PICTURE

*"You're only as good as what you leave behind
when you leave this world."*

"Dream a dream that has no point of reference."

**ROSA PORTO, CO-FOUNDER OF
PORTO'S CUBAN BAKERY**

I have a "Picture of the Day," an image I select and hold onto for twenty-four hours. I find these pics everywhere—on billboards, in magazine articles and books, on-line. They might be pictures I've taken—I'm an avid amateur photographer. I got hooked long ago when the camera lens taught me that I determine what I focus on and that it can be memorialized. Pictures make me smile. They make me aware of details surrounding me that I'd otherwise miss or take for granted.

It's the same with God. He created this entire universe for us. When we don't acknowledge the beauty of His creation, the careful attention to each and every detail, when we take this creation for granted, I wonder how that makes Him feel? Acknowledging the small details is my way of acknowledging how big our God is.

It's the same as walking past something that you drive past daily. Walking causes us to slow down and take in details that we miss when flying by. Training the heart to look and lead from a place of joy requires slowing down to look for the details in the simplest and grandest things that we've been failing to fully appreciate. With fresh eyes comes a fresh perspective. These are the seeds of appreciation that influence our gratitude.

When you pay attention and acknowledge what you've been missing, you can't help but see items to add to your gratitude list (I keep a list and add to it at the end of each day), you can't help but grow and allow joy to come forth. Things that once seemed seriously important are rearranged and lose their grip on you. You're freer to see and to believe. The growing gratitude list causes me to pray and creates a desire to experience more contentment within the day-to-day moments of life. Watching a child hold a door open for someone on crutches struggling to balance bags of groceries reminds us that kindness prevails, despite the battles of the world. Overhearing an apology softens us to be more patient. Seeing the thousands of containers at the San Pedro Port 'O Call reminds me of resources others go without. Staring at wind surfers being lifted into the air by the winds of a stormy sea can be a breathtaking reminder that there's truly a way to seize every opportunity as a way to harness the good around us.

Pray and praise are the natural order of gratitude. So is living from a place of joy, even in the turbulent moments. I have moments when random thoughts run through my mind the way pictures slide across my computer screensaver throughout the day. These mental images are snapshots of moments that have lingered with me, sometimes for hours, even years. They make me smile, feel encouraged, inspired, hopeful, thankful. To create more of these moments, I capture snapshots I've taken in the most random of circumstances, when my eye catches a glimpse of someone or something I want to record within my heart.

To create beautiful memories, I need images to help me memorialize the daily moments I otherwise would have neglected. This makes me more intentional in how I see others and the good around me. I have some of these cherished images framed and hung throughout out home. They're also printed on clothing, carry-on luggage, paper I use as book covers, stationery, cards, and mugs. This practice of looking for the good around me and the importance of capturing it in photographs has made me increase and value the mental images that confirm it. This practice has been reaffirmed during funeral services, especially for those whom I loved that were elderly. I marvel at how well-preserved images capture a life just shy of a century. I appreciate how they tell an inspirational story of everyday moments. Inspirational moments happen all the time and they happen fast. They're over before you know it. Take a snapshot of that moment in your mind or with your camera, or tear it out of a magazine. Whatever the source, in any given moment, each pic may be the *one*, that special one that reappears in your random thoughts in the future. That one photo of that one moment could be what keeps you looking for the good surrounding you.

This lesson was reaffirmed recently when I was on a Skype training call with smiling young university students in their dormitories who were sharing common university experiences of exams, long nights at the library, time with friends, and food. From France to China, Africa to Kyrgyzstan, Afghanistan to Claremont, California—everyone found something in common. Their intellectual conversations and the images of their smiling faces will always be with me. But it was the image shared by two of the young ladies in Kabul, Afghanistan, that will forever stay with me as a Picture of the Day. It was a candid photo of their families on a Sunday picnic in what they referenced casually as one of the many beautiful parks throughout Afghanistan.

How could one of the recent most war-torn countries in the world have beautiful parks? And how could these people be smiling? That's what I wanted to know. They looked so normal for living in such abnormal circumstances. When I couldn't hold the question back any longer, I asked about the smiles, and, in unison, the young ladies said, "Because we choose to." Then they nodded, affirming that *Yes. It's true. We don't know if we'll live or die or if our family will, so we choose to smile.* They choose to create memories that fuel their joy and propel them to capture every opportunity. They embrace all of life. We have the ability to experience the same, and to express ourselves through images we carry with us. When someone looks at one of our photos, they can see that moment exactly the way we did. Photography can convey unspoken ideas hidden within our souls in very artistic, visual, and creative ways.

We relive so many memoires through photos. I'm sure you've said something like, "I remember this!" or "We had so much fun here!" It didn't matter that the photos were probably taken by an amateur photographer on a Polaroid or on an iPhone. The photos did the job of capturing those memories.

There's always an image that's a part of our self-talk, and we can choose which images to focus on. These images prompt other sensory details. For example, when I catch myself thinking about a conversation over dim sum with friends and family, I'm reliving everything about that moment. The visuals—the restaurant decor, how everyone looked, bite-sized treats nestled in steamer baskets.

These visuals trigger sounds—our laughter (and what made us laugh), individual voices, the background noise of chairs scraping, the low hum of conversation, the door opening and closing. And winding through it all is a narrative of the experience of being with good friends while eating a delicious meal: *That's why dim sum means "touch the heart."* I refill my sense of hopefulness and joy with the smile these memories bring and my own internal narrative weaving through my thoughts, lifting my self-talk.

On the other hand, if the image I hold within me focuses on a troubling conversation, circumstance, or experience, then throughout the day I'm depleted by fear or disappointment or anger, if that is the dominant fuel source. Negative distractions turn my thoughts away from the good around me. So, I consciously choose an image that upholds the feeling I'm desiring, the details of good around me. Sometimes this is a simple image that I've taken with my cell phone of a yellow hibiscus flower. Other times it's an image I found on the Internet. I have one (among many) on my computer screen of an elderly couple who gave birth to a baby recently. She was seventy-two and he was seventy-nine. A real live Abraham and Sarah story. After forty-six years of trying to conceive, she underwent IVF and the embryo (consisting of a donor's egg and her husband's sperm) was implanted into her womb. She physically gave birth. The picture of these elderly parents is a profound reminder of expecting the unexpected, which is why it's become one of my favorite choices for my Picture of the Day.

Talk about an image that will help carry me forward, no matter what I'm birthing! The power of the image helps shape self-thoughts and perspectives through the day. It helps me to be more patient, more joyful, more peaceful, and I believe it can do the same for you.

I encourage you to get out your phone or your camera and go capture some memories! Let your Picture of the Day be a way you give thanks, your head-nod or wink to acknowledge seeing something good that you don't want to take for granted. Let the image be one that makes you feel good. You may find them on the Internet or in magazines, coming from the cracks in the sidewalk, architecture, nature. Make it your scavenger hunt to look intentionally, capture the smallest details within the daily moments that are a special way to say "Thank you. I see you." Have a "Theme Picture of the Day", the week, the month, the year! Go capture the moments that happen around you! Tell stories with your images! Use them as screensavers on your computer, magnets on your refrigerator, calendars, post-it notes, mouse pads. I have a personal philosophy of wanting every space that I look upon to make me smile. From the color on the wall to the paper napkins and lining in bathroom drawers. The good around me is in the details.

I hope and pray that by opening the eyes of your heart to acknowledge the good around you, you too can continually improve, can sensitize yourself by expanding and opening to the creation around you.

Songs OF THE DAY

God Is
JAMES CLEVELAND

Ain't No Way
ARETHA FRANKLIN

CONFIDENCE
THROUGH FAILURE

"Be yourself, everyone else is taken."

OSCAR WILDE

It's amazing what failure can teach you. Your failures can teach you lessons about relationships, yourself, your misplaced priorities, your strengths, your weaknesses, and your areas of opportunity. Failures can also bring you into your greater good.

Yes. I know a few things about failure and the power it contains to bring forth an abundance of good that I would have otherwise missed. During a business cocktail hour, I listened to a conversation in which two men shared a story about a series of interviews conducted by a prominent board of directors for a major corporation. Their search for the right CEO attracted the best, with the traditional Ivy League pedigree. Academic degrees in hand, each candidate had social and educational connections that proved worthy of making the final round of interviews. The defining question the board asked each candidate at the end of the round of questioning was this: "Tell us about your biggest failure." More often than not, all were embarrassed to acknowledge that they could have possibly failed at anything, so each hid their failures and boasted of their accomplishments. Just as the board members were growing weary of the process, another candidate appeared. His qualifications proved worthy of an interview, even though he was less competitive in other areas due to noticeable gaps in his career path following his academic training.

At the end of questioning, the board said to the man, "Talk to us about your biggest failure." He seemed to slump slightly in his chair before quickly regaining his composure. He paused, placed his folded hands on the table, and looked each corporate leader in the eye. "Well, before that first gap in my resume, I started a business. I had a very clear vision of what I was to be doing and I set out to make it happen, but the business folded. I didn't have enough wisdom at that time to know what I didn't know, until it seemed too late to recover. The great part was that I had made wonderful contacts, so I had sought out the skills of others and learned from the best."

He continued to share his story without being able to interpret the facial expressions of the interviewers, who kept their expressions intentionally neutral. "In my quest to succeed in that business, I neglected my family. I had no idea I was being negligent. I justified all the hard work I put into the business as being a good provider for my family. That business didn't make it either. Just as my business was falling apart, so did my marriage. The stress took a toll on my health. The loss of business income also cost me my home. I took time to heal and recover. Thus the next gap in my resume."

"Here's the good news." He perked up. "That healing time was reflective time. I was able to come face-to-face with my own behaviors and to make an honest effort to recalibrate my life and my relationships. I never gave up on my dream to run a successful company and to be a good provider to my family. I wanted to honor my wedding vows that included, 'for richer or for poorer.' I reworked my business plan by including the best-of-the-best from lessons I'd learned earlier.

"I utilized all of the resources I had at hand. Day-by-day I began with a renewed commitment to succeed based on new definitions of success. Failure feels shameful. But I had to face it—my business had failed. I saw the gaps in my own thinking, my misplaced priorities, and where I needed help. I changed my perspective with the intentional hope that the next time around things would in fact be different. My priorities shifted. With a spirit of gratitude I began to create a new life. I was able to convince my wife to not give up on me. My gratitude for a family that didn't abandon me aided in my healthy recovery. The gap between experiencing failure and recovering was a period of healing. This healing would eventually lead to renewal. That third gap on my resume, that time of renewal, was followed by rebuilding and selling the company for an amount exceeding my original plans."

The board had been advised to interview this gentleman because he was regarded as a successful businessman with similar core values based on his life and business experiences. He made a choice to learn from his "failures." Little did he know this distinguished group of business leaders had had periods of perceived failures on their path to greatness. They saw a peer sitting before them. They felt they could trust his transparency in questionable moments. They could trust his integrity when given responsibilities where failure was possible. They hired him.

Own all of life's opportunities, the good, the bad, the ugly, the ups and the downs. Learn from the full ride of life: The failures, the successes, and the disappointments while waiting for future outcomes to prove you right. Our son uses an expression, "Game recognizes game." In other words, people who have game (skill/ excellence), recognize it and respect it in others. In other words, "It takes one to know one." These gifted board members recognized game in this candidate.

The universe is full of surprises. You never know where or when those gifts may appear or from whom. You are never alone. There will be others who have a deeper understanding of who you are and your potential. They will be looking for you. In some cases, it actually feels like they were waiting for your arrival. When that divine appointment happens, you'll feel ready. You will be ready for the bigger opportunity and good that you had dreamed of to come forth. Your priorities will align with your purpose. When we go it alone, all can seem lost. Be encouraged to hold on. Be strong. Three of the advantages of knowing you're never alone on your life's journey are that (1) you can learn from others, (2) you can gain access to people and knowledge that will aid you in your accomplishments, and (3) you'll realize you were created for success, so you know you always have help with the goals you set.

I believe that God has many blessings in store for you! I believe that you were not a mistake and that you were created with favor for specific work, and that no one else can do what you were born to do or be who you were born to be. With this in mind, surely there's favor in your future like you've never imagined. No matter where I've lived or what rocky paths I've traveled, I have clung to the belief that God wants to take us places that neither you nor I ever even dreamed. But for us to experience all these blessings, we have to increase our capacity to receive.

Think about this one last story. If you have a one-gallon bucket and someone has fifty gallons to give you, the problem is not with the supply. The problem is that you don't have the capacity to receive the fifty gallons. But if you get yourself a larger container, then you will be able to receive more.

It's the same way with God. If we think we've reached our limit, the problem isn't that God doesn't have the resources or the ability. The problem is that our human container is too small. We have to enlarge our vision and make room for the new things God has for us. I'm finding that there are God-size holes in my thinking, experiences, and abilities. These holes require me to do all I can to be intentional in filling them with words of encouragement, routines, and relationships that pour goodness and kindness into the spaces that otherwise would be painful and fuel discouragement. The ritual of expressing gratitude at the beginning and end of each day makes it possible to close these holes of despair. Writing these words down creates forever reminders that wherever I go His goodness will prevail. When I have that kind of attitude, I'm increasing my capacity to receive so I can live the abundant life He has in store for me to share with others.

I encourage you to have faith. Know what your financial options are and be assured that if you believe that you have failed, you are now able to believe that you, too, will recover. Anticipate good. First, you have to choose to believe it. Then you have to choose to see it. Finally, you have to choose to connect with it.

It's my hope and prayer that who you are meant to be starts from where you are right this moment. Seeing obstacles for what they are will keep you from losing faith. Mistakes? Setbacks? New beginnings? All are a part of the tools you can utilize to create the greatest of work art ever—your life!

Song OF THE DAY

Came to My Rescue
HILLSONG

BE STILL

"Not all those who wander are lost."

J.R. TOLKIEN, *LORD OF THE RINGS*

"The thing that frustrates me about my parents," my friend sitting across from me in Starbucks said, "is that they are always on my back about the craziest things—like wanting me to meet and marry a man with the same faith beliefs that I have... wanting me to start a business...wanting me to see the world... wanting me to live my best life. I could be worse. I could be on drugs or in jail! Now that would be something to complain about. I'm just trying to do me."

As this young single mother bemoaned the pressures of trying to please her hard-to-please parents, my thoughts turned to the Whitney Houston song "One Moment In Time." That's all we have each day—one moment in time. The moments accumulate.

Meeting with my friend in my neighborhood Starbucks wasn't my first choice (it was so loud), but it was better than texting. Still, I tried to listen carefully, be fully present in the moment, but the sounds around me kept grabbing my attention, making it impossible to fully engage. The song playing over the sound system instantly transported me to memories of people and places who hadn't walked into Starbucks with me. While in the present, I watched a boyfriend and girlfriend argue over what time to meet Kristin and where, only to be distracted by the doting father a few tables over shouting over the din as he recited the ingredients of the Vermont maple muffin to his ten-month-old. The guy next to us on his cellphone with his mother was stressing about a looming deadline for an MBA program.

My friend's back was to all of this, so I tried to disguise my distraction by gazing her way. *Man!!!* I thought. *This is crazy how other people's behavior can be a such a distraction, it's even crazier that acting this ways seems so reasonable to them that no one else matters.* While we talked, I couldn't help paying attention to everyone except the person right in front me, *That child doesn't know where Vermont is or the difference between agave and maple, but we're supposed to make it a priority to care how cute your adorable child is and what a well-informed child he will be because of this moment? And Kristin?! Who is Kristin and why do we have to hear you yell at each other? Oh my gosh! Pay attention, G.S.! Be present!* These private thoughts came from out of nowhere, an unexpected guest in a private conversation. How private can our conversation be when it's in a public space with chairs close enough to share the table with others?

I was trying to be in the moment. I *was* trying. Truly trying to listen, to be present for my friend. But I found myself stuck. I was suddenly back in my own memories and my own MBA conversation. The rapid-fire memories associated with voices of support and the silence in conversations from years gone by returned to invade the quiet places where I'd left them after getting a BA. My friend was wrapped up in the sound of her own voice. Unexpectedly, I was wrapped up in the silence of hurt from years gone by.

For many years, my secret longings included getting a dual MBA and law degree. Although I had no interest in practicing law, I desired the knowledge. But if the thought of facing my fear of numbers wasn't a sufficient excuse, I could always fall back on age, mortgage obligations, a young child, and a car in need of replacement as understandable reasons not to proceed. Well, the young child went off to college, the mortgage obligations of our first home were replaced with investment properties, and many new model cars were parked in our garage over the years. The many years!

It wasn't until our son was a freshman in college that I shared with him my aspiration. Perhaps it was the maternal adjustment to that new empty nest chapter of life, but my desire was real—I had a moment in life to do and be more. It was time to dream new impossible dreams and explore the feelings pushing to the forefront of my thoughts. The power of our son's kind words was sufficient for me to reach out to the dean of a local law school that a close friend had attended as a young mother with several children. She never practiced law but shared her knowledge via community involvement on boards. She'd attended law school partly to satisfy her personal goal of just knowing she could do it!

My husband encouraged me. Our son encouraged me. It didn't take a lot of words, just a listening ear and honesty from their open loving hearts. The few words spoken were words of encouragement: "I know you will do very well. You already do the legal work for our businesses and family. You can read the temperature of business health from a P&L the way you read a thermometer when someone has a fever. We understand why you waited so long, but no need to wait any longer. Do it! We're proud of you!"

Empowered by my hopes and their encouragement, I also shot off two emails to publishers regarding book concepts I'd been carrying around long enough to have birthed at least ten more children. I just did it! No second-guessing. No apprehension. I wrote them and clicked SEND.

I then contacted the dean of the law school. She enthusiastically encouraged me to let her give me a tour and to apply. She said she would also let our mutual friend know so that she could add support and insight about successfully crossing the finish line. I was so excited! Oh my gosh! This could finally possibly happen? Glimpses of my younger shy self as a senior in college suddenly appeared. That year I'd felt I was the only one of my peers who was undecided about next steps. I cheered others forward as they submitted their applications to graduate schools, medical schools, and law schools, never revealing my own longing to apply.

Where had all that insecurity come from? The many moments filled with words of discouragement from others? Words that pierced and stuck with me? How many needles do you have to have sticking within you to feel the sting of pain? Removing ten might lessen the intensity, but it couldn't relieve the ache caused by the remaining one. Sometimes it's hard fighting the good fight forward.

As I prepared to meet the dean, I reminded myself of all my blessings (and they were many), all my accomplishments (and they, too, were many). I felt nervously excited. My enthusiasm caused me to call my friend before the dean did. Excited beyond words, I spilled out my intentions to finally go to law school.

I smiled as I remembered her sharing the joyful celebration her family and friends had for her the day she graduated.

Anticipating enthusiasm for the day I would graduate from the same law school, I was stunned when she filled this one moment in time with these words: "Why on earth would you want to do that?! You're already successful in business! Your son is at a prestigious university! You have no idea how hard it is! It doesn't make any sense for you to go to law school at this stage in life! What are you going to do, compete with the younger grads for jobs?" On and on and on she fired, blasting my dream, my sacred dream, to tiny pieces. I don't remember how the conversation concluded. Perhaps my silence caused her to think we had been disconnected. Perhaps I just hung up. I only remember leaning against the wall and crying. Crying.

I don't remember how long I stayed in that spot, gulping back sobs. I never told her how hurtful and disappointing her words were. I just went on with my life. That same day I received two encouraging emails from the publishers asking me to forward more information! Wow! Through blurry eyes, I thought about how it's just so hard it is to be a wife, a mom, a friend, and all those other people I could also be. Regardless of my age, experience, and a multitude of reasons to proceed, I never responded to them. I cancelled the tour of the law school too. I stopped my crying and went back to work.

Fourteen years and two grandchildren later, along with the thousands of miles between that day and the day in Starbucks, I listened to the frustrated, whining young mother, which was all she was asking of me—to listen. But I wanted to shout, "Stop your whining! Stop trying to change your parents and get up and do what you want to do with your life! You've got one moment in time when you can be more than you thought you could be. Start with being still." But I didn't. I've learned that if I am to "Just do it!" the first thing I need to do is to be still within. I can't change how my former friend reacted. I can't change the actions of everyone around me, but I can center myself and just be rather than react.

It had taken more than fourteen years of opportunities to practice stillness in chaos. But I knew how to find it. I looked for it. I sought a change in perspective within the moment. I couldn't change where Kristin showed up or if that doting father would learn to be considerate with voice volume, but I could find a quiet place within my thoughts to bring me back to the peaceful places of the moment. So in my neighborhood Starbucks, I stopped my thoughts of criticism. I whispered a prayer of success for the young man at the next table and his grad school application. I found a heart-space that put everyone around me on mute, because I was truly thankful that my friend wasn't in jail or on drugs and that with her MBA she blesses and inspires me because she is trusting me with her words. I listen.

I wanted to tell the whining young mother in this moment a truth spoken by C. G. Jung when he said, "Nothing has a stronger influence psychologically on their environment and especially on their children than the unlived life of the parent." Within my stillness, those fourteen years ago, I learned the importance of consciously creating a psychological environment based on my faith in Christ, to live as a parent who influences belief in great outcomes. I learned that it's important to be the friend to myself that I hoped she would have been to me. I took steps to preserve hope. Although I have successfully pursued other dreams and not the law degree or MBA (yet), I believe that the voice that spoke the loudest to my heart was to listen for guidance in multiple experiences. I desired the same for this young mother.

I eventually spoke. I told her to "Be the parent that you wanted your parents to be! Take a first step and then a second. Stop talking to others about it! Stop hoping they will change and be what you need and want them to be. It's not about them. It's about you! What will you do with this moment? Whine and complain? Cry? Ponder? Question? Give up? No!! You will choose to look for the good around you and to ponder it in quietness. Then get up! All of your dreams are a heartbeat away and the answers are all up to you. You'll rise and fall, yet through it all this much remains: you can't change others to be what you want them to be. You can only choose to believe and to do something to encourage your soul! Go do the laundry! Go do what you must do for now, but also *go* to work and make sure you work on choosing to seize that one moment in time, even if it takes many moments to get you there. Choose to do something. From a quiet place and daily practices of inspiration, choose to meet new people. Choose new friends. Choose to take new steps within the moment."

I did just that. I realigned my friendships. And you're reading an excerpt from one of the books that I'd queried publishers about so long ago. It's not too late for me to choose law school, but I'm certainly choosing to enjoy the journey with those who enrich each moment by encouraging others.

Starting today, I encourage you to get still within. Whether the voices come from within your private thoughts or from others in a Starbucks, practice finding by acknowledging, blessing, and releasing. Start now.

It's my hope and prayer that you'll be encouraged just knowing that a random stranger is taking this one moment in time to write, "I'm writing these words to you, cheering you forward, and believing you're closer than you realize. Expand your belief in bigger possibilities. Good is waiting to become a part of your life story.

Songs OF THE DAY

Start Me Up
ROLLING STONES

I Dreamed a Dream
SUSAN BOYLE

CONTENTMENT DAY

"May your word to me be fulfilled."

LUKE, 1:38

*"Hope begins in the dark, the stubborn hope that
if you just show up and try to do the right thing,
the dawn will come. You wait and watch and work:
you don't give up."*

ANNE LAMOTT, *BIRD BY BIRD*

Graduation Day! It can be an exhilarating time filled with as many emotional and mental trips as a Christmas fruitcake. Whether you like it or not, the combination of all the elements—whether it's the general education requirements you saw no point to or the mixture of candied fruit—somehow eventually makes sense. A graduating college senior recently called me and asked, "What are the five most important insights you can share with a graduating senior from college? Insights about succeeding in a career?"

In my response to her, I learned that I was the one who needed advice.

1. AVOID JUDGMENT

This young woman always seemed to exude a self-confidence that could be misinterpreted as arrogance. Before I answered her question, I asked, "How are you feeling about your upcoming graduation and returning home?"

Her four years had been filled with more international travel than most people experience in a lifetime, even those who are accomplished globe-trotting retirees. She seemed to "have it all": intellect, physical beauty, boyfriend, reputation as a fashionista, resources, and a hint of Christian faith experiences buried somewhere in there. Her answer to my question did more than surprise me, it quieted my internal voices of judgment. "I'm scared," she said.

"What scares you most?" I asked.

"Fear of the unknown. Leaving my friends. The fear of not knowing what I'm doing. I was hoping you might help me?"

Well, if you haven't gained a glimpse into my heart by this time, let this be an opportunity for you to learn more about me. Tears filled my eyes. I wanted to hug her and reassure her that all would be a glorious adventure and the future was waiting with open arms to carry her forward in amazing ways, that all that she had been through and gained from the previous four years would serve her well. But first, I wanted to say, "I'm sorry for my small thoughts toward you and the big mistake I made in assuming anything about you that tripped you up by the tangles of my own mind." I wanted to ask her to please forgive me. I was not only wrong about her; I was grossly mistaken. I wanted to let her know that I had been wanting to get to know her so that I could *truly* know her, so I could dispel my prejudgments.

My tears washed away the residual first impressions as I listened sincerely to her heart. The words she shared were those of forgiveness. Her grace and mercy filled my heart and gave me a new understanding of both and why they're essential for all humanity. In my silence, I thanked her. In response to her openness, I opened up and shared these tips with her as the best I could in the absence of a hug in person. May I learn from her as much as I'm learning about myself.

"First," I said," summing up the lesson I'd just revisited in my assumptions about her, "know that judging others can be harmful and harm depletes us of joy." Then I moved to the next item on the list.

2. USE JOY AS YOUR BAROMETER

Let joy be the barometer keeping you on track. Even in the midst of dark confusion, pain, and loss. Seek a place of peace that helps your heart to see what He sees and hear what He hears. Happiness is fleeting. Joy is foundational. This doesn't mean you'll always be skipping, whistling, and dancing in the rain. It does mean that because you make a habit of cultivating peace of mind grounded in faith that you are creating within yourself a place as comfortable with waiting as with seeing something through. You can find within a quiet space where your thoughts can find rest. In the presence of chaos and mind-boggling issues, you can go to your room within and breathe to quiet your restless soul. For me, the practice of gratitude requires the eyes of my heart to search diligently for signs of any goodness within the moments. Yes! That includes emergency circumstances at an ER or grouchy irritable people we thought would be helpful but add to the aggravation or the discomfort of a conversation. All of those crazy bad moments are surrounded by something that I can cry out to God to help me see.

3. COMPROMISE

My third piece of advice to this young woman was: don't compromise in your relationships. But this doesn't mean you're unwilling to seek neutral ground or compromise in specific circumstances. Bring a spirit of loving compromise when needed. But don't feel that you ever have to settle for less than you believe God would offer to you as the best. Be watchful that negative patterns don't form and you find yourself surrounded by a person, or people, of diverging ethics, beliefs, behaviors, words, deeds who transfer their expectations to you. There are some people you won't belong with, and some places you won't belong in. Learn to recognize that and to accept it.

You are not a square peg needing to force yourself into any round holes. Whether a love relationship, acquaintance friendship, or work relationship — don't get caught up in others' perceptions of what you should tolerate in a relationship. Don't let others define what is good for you. Within a relationship, be what you desire the other person to be. Bring compassion. Bring your best self. Bring forgiveness. Love listening. Love learning. Be in relationships you love.

Be patient with yourself. Because within your best self is the less-than-the-best you. So bring patience. Lots of patience and openness. Bring patience for yourself as your relationships help you grow. Growth is good when it is healthy growth. In situations in life, unhealthy people will cross your path. Don't let them stay. Allow them to keep moving on. Be willing to learn and to understand. It's not always about me. It is about the "us" in relationships. Both of you have to be healthy to form an "us." Seek, encourage, and desire the best for others.

4. OBSERVE

Look at the elements of joy reflected within the lives of others. Perhaps it's the long hours dedicated to a task that makes someone happy that encourages you also to seek a life experience that you can immerse yourself in. Or it's a lifestyle choice that made no sense but eventually opened doors to other opportunities. Life isn't linear for many of us. Don't be afraid of the crooked paths that twist and turn in inexplicably odd ways. Look ahead at the lives of people ten, twenty, forty-plus years older and glean the wisdom that will help you choose a direction your heart will seek to follow. Look at the practical. Consider it wisely. At the same time, embrace the impractical and allow it to make you laugh. Look closely at what breaks up relationships, what causes loss and pain, and how people manage to make it through. Look closely at the successful steps and the missteps of others. Learn. Watch and learn. Apply and try. Finding your way does not always require doing it alone. Look for what's noble. Look for the good and what's right. Look for the purity and the beauty in others and around you. Whatever's admirable, whatever's excellent or worth you smiling and praising. Do just as Philippians 4:8–9 wisely advises — think about such things. Whatever you have learned or received or heard from me, or seen in me—put into practice. And the God of peace will be with you.

I struggle periodically with the promise that the God of peace will be with me, that if I let the Lord Jesus Christ and the Holy Spirit fill me and transform my heart and mind, abundant life will be offered to me—I trust in Him. I continue to seek courage to always choose what is good, true, and just and to reject whatever is false, foolish, and contrary to His holy will.

5. AIM FOR CONTENTMENT

In the midst of my periodic spiritual struggles, I begin easing into mental and emotional states of satisfaction in every situation. It is there that contentment appears. Not the kind of contentment that justifies my limiting my desires, as John Stuart Mills encouraged.

Not the contentment that comes from giving up and just accepting intolerable circumstances when things feel out of my control or beyond my grasp, but a sense of a tentative form of happiness. Health is a precious resource and contentment a valuable possession. I know from personal circumstances and numerous observations that contentment is not solely determined by finances or the exclusive striving to secure any specific thing we perceive to have more value than it actually has.

There are some religious beliefs, including those held by some Christian denominations, that throw life and the pursuit of happiness out of balance by emphasizing these words found in Hebrews 13:5: "Keep your lives free from the love of money and be content with what you have, because God has said, 'Never will I leave you; never will I forsake you.'" No one can define how much is too much or when too little for one person is just the right amount for another. Our family had a long discussion about this once after sitting through yet another sermon about how much easier it is for a camel to go through the eye of a needle than it is for the rich man to go to heaven. This was a common theme of the sermons of a particular pastor in Ohio, and Mark and I could anticipate her turning any message, on any topic to this particular theme: Rich people are bad; poor people are good.

The bigger challenge for us was that she was also the one who would call us like clockwork each year for us to host the all-church breakfast, along with another member who was a business partner of ours. We were left wanting to ask her, "So this time each year our wealth is good and the remainder of the year our wealth, address, or vehicle categorize us as hell-bound?" There's so much more to us than meets the judging eye. Like many others, we kept the conversation to ourselves.

The flip side was seeing a man standing on island next to a left-hand turn lane, exposed to the blazing Arizona sun and holding a cardboard sign with the message "Help, please. I'm homeless. Need food." By all outward appearances he was clean shaven, tidy, and able-bodied, but I didn't want that observation to be the basis for my judging him and not responding. As is one of my customary responses, I waited for the light to change and planned to hand him both water and money once I was closer.

That didn't happen. He passed three closer vehicles as he rushed toward my car, yelling, "*You* better give me some money driving a big expensive car like that!"

"I'd *better!?*"

He didn't know me or my circumstances any more than I knew his, beyond what he advertised about himself.

That was a defining moment for me: *Nobody* gets to define who I am, what I'm capable of doing, and who or how I make the most of my life! Nobody. That includes being content whether I have much or little—and as with the reference to the eye of the needle, *that's also scriptural.* There's a Japanese word, *monku*, that our family uses when we find ourselves muttering or whining. As Paul says, "I am not saying this because I am in need, for I have learned to be content whatever the circumstances." (Philippians 4:11) After years living in Ohio and Arizona, where our conditions were as extremely different through the years as the winters are between the two, I had to remind myself to stop my monku and be content regardless of outward appearances and what others may have thought.

Chinese philosopher Zhuang Zhou is credited with once writing, "A gentleman who profoundly penetrates all things and is in harmony with their transformations will be contented with whatever time may bring. He follows the course of nature in whatever situation he may be."

It's generally agreed that contentment is maybe a state ideally reached through being happy with what a person has, as opposed to achieving one's larger ambitions. Happiness is a passing state that can indicate that I'm heading in a good direction to experience joy. Graduating to a place of contentment, free from the self-imposed pressure of trying to always please others, includes gratitude. Gratitude is a key element of achievement that may make finding a state of personal contentment easier. Appreciation for all things big and small, simple and extravagant—a strong family unit, a strong local community, and satisfaction of life's basic needs, which includes smiles, hugs, peace, laughter, food, music, and more. I think that the wisdom of old is as relevant today as it was then, and I want to emphasize how important it is for you to be content with what you have in this moment because that will help ensure you'll be content with what you would like to have.

What graduation day in life experiences would be confirmed without contentment? We must be content with our accomplishments and lessons learned that have brought us to this point. Within this moment, we're pausing to acknowledge the goodness of all we've observed, experienced, and released. Today, if I'm not recognizing the fullness of my abundant life, it's because there are moments when I fail to be content with what I have.

Contentment. When is enough, enough? My life is joy-filled, loving, healthy, and beautiful. Answered prayers surround me. What more do I need and what more do I want? The answer? Gratitude for all I have and the honor of being blessed to dream for more for others.

These are the five things I shared with this young woman and would share with anyone preparing to launch into adulthood.

I encourage you to experience the unmistakable freedom of contentment. I encourage you to break the habit of attempting to satisfy your discontent with acquisitions, unhealthy relationships, and other poor substitutes that distract you from living a life of joy. Your contentment is not dependent upon your acquisition of any possession. It's solely a choice to be intentional about an attitude of thanksgiving. It begins with gratitude for who you are, what you do have, and the seeds you plant within your thoughts, words you speak, and what you choose to fill yourself with. From where you are right now, you can grow into so much more. Start with a written list at the top of your calendar of ten things you're grateful for and your "To Do List." Make being grateful a "To Do." Add ten more new items at the close of the day. Repeat this with the same commitment you make to eating and exercising as an aid in your overall health. Read and write your gratitude list before, during, or following these essential daily activities.

It's my hope and prayer for you that if you find this challenging when you first start, you'll learn to look with ease at the smallest detail around you that makes you feel good and persist. Soon, when you review your list, you'll find that it exceeds your expectations for what you actually do have to be grateful for.

PART

III

IGNITING A SENSE OF *faith*

Every day, we're provided with a gift of selecting the best or most appropriate of two or more alternative thoughts. We can choose to have a conviction of hope from morning to evening. Or not. And there's another gift: the choice of living and leading from a place of joy, because we choose to put our faith in the good outcomes rather than the alternative. Optimism is a choice. It's the kindling that will set our hearts on fire to experience more goodness and joy. It's the spark that could be enough to set our faith ablaze. Now is the time to fan the flickering flame, to keep the light burning and to be reassured that it won't go out. Choosing faith and optimism is especially important during the joyless moments if we want to be reassured that we will, indeed, get through tough times.

For My Sister
AI NO KO

THE IMPERFECT PLAN FOR THE REST OF MY LIFE

"Dream a dream that has no point of reference."

GSP

The rest of my life is the best of my life and it starts right now.

Being of Christian faith, I often hear and read about God having a perfect plan and that all things are working together for good. There is truth in these words and I do believe them. *But...* I can't help but ponder why I feel relief when I manage my expectations, when I try to do things from a place of human logic and not in faith. If I leave my expectations within the realm of normal, rational, realistic goal-setting, I can surround myself with a larger community of like-minded small thinkers and dreamers, and there can be justification to stay in those warm fuzzy places. But that gets uncomfortable for me. It's like a pair of pants gets uncomfortable around the waist after you've consumed too much of the wrong food—a squeezing pressure that means something's going to pop, something's got to give.

It's hard to live small when the world of opportunities is so big. It's hard not to believe in impossible when you've experienced the impossible time and time again. So why do we manage our expectations and stay small? Because if we expect small, we don't risk experiencing big disappointments, right? If I didn't have this crazy faith that there's a perfect plan for my life—no matter what my life looks like at any moment—and that anything's possible, I might very well want to manage my expectations. Without that crazy faith in a perfect plan, I'd be freaked out by the infinite unimaginable possibilities in store for me. I imagine it would feel much safer to create a strict life plan with the aim of living a familiar version of what's called "perfectly normal." But you know what they say, "When man plans, God laughs." When we operate from a place of confidence that things are going to work out okay, we can predict with absolute certainty that something unexpected will show up. My challenge has been learning to relax within the imperfect moments of life.

I have extreme faith and belief in a positive outcome, faith that often appears illogical to the rational mind. I believed I would return to cycling long distances and start dancing competitively when I was partially immobilized by a back injury and had never danced competitively before. I believed this with a crazy, hard-to-explain faith. Every physician I consulted concluded—independently of one another—that I needed surgery. And the optimum expected outcome of that surgery? Slow strolls. There's a part of me that sometimes throws my hands up when caught in these imperfect moments, not in frustration, but as a gesture of letting go of the expected outcomes when things appear to fall apart. But with my back, I didn't throw up my hands. I just knew what I knew. I was going to dance. I was going to ride long distances. I had no doubt.

Perhaps I've had enough time and been through enough circumstances to see the domino effect of these events, to trust that all things work together for good and beyond my wildest expectations. My faith gave me the ability to heal my back without surgery. The doctors I'd consulted were at a loss for an explanation when, less than three months later, I was back in the gym, came in first place in my second community cycling event, and won multiple First Place prizes (in two states!) for dancing. These types of experiences exceed wishful thinking. They are the result of a steadfast faith in the face of harsh realities that have stopped many. In each instance, I could have chosen not to believe and to ignore the inner voice asking me to trust and believe, or I could choose to believe. Each time I go through these crazy circumstances where I choose to believe, where I hold fast to my faith, I experience a deeper knowing of what is meant to be true.

As much as I'd like to have access to a perfect plan, one where I can see how all events unfold, the timing, dependencies, outcomes, end dates, I've never known that to work. If I can't have the perfect plan laid out in front of me, at the very least I'd like a perfect understanding of both personal and business decisions I've made that seemed counter-intuitive. There have been times I've heeded my inner voice and made the counter-intuitive choice, only to switch to the more seemingly logical solution, only to later learn I had in fact been heading in a right direction and what appeared to be failure was not failure, but movement toward a plan. Just not the one I'd envisioned. Better. For example, when I was faced with the choice between paying the tuition and book fees for someone else's child and covering my utilities, groceries, and mortgage, I chose the child. In response, God, or, as some would say, the Universe, chose miraculous responses to take care of my needs. My back healing is another example. As much as I'd like to have glimpses into the much bigger perfect plan, my life experiences thus far indicate that won't be happening unless I remember the moments that the miraculous happened.

Sometimes I get just enough of a glimpse to reaffirm my faith, to stir up a spirit of resilience and a song to get up and keep going. Moments such as Girls Fly! Compton, when I didn't know anyone or anything about Compton, yet I announced to a standing-room-only conference room at the Warner Bros. studio office in Burbank that "I had a 3:15 am wake-up call from God saying, 'It's not Hollywood or Monrovia just yet. It's Compton. Girls Fly! Compton. We are to go to Compton.'" I told them we were shifting program and marketing plans for the national launch of Girls Fly! to focus on a community we hadn't even considered—Compton, not Hollywood or Monrovia, as we'd planned for more than two years.

When God first said "Compton," I thought I'd heard incorrectly. It didn't make logical sense. Compton? Why would we completely change cities after two years of planning? Why was I just hearing about this new plan now? Unexpectedly, during the ninety-minute drive from my house to Burbank, two things happened that gave me a glimpse into a bigger plan. First, Walter Hawkins's song "Never Alone" came on the radio. I hadn't heard that song in more than ten years. The lyrics reminded me that I don't have to worry. I'm never alone. Listen to it. You'll hear what I heard and I hope that you, too, will know that there are times when the path ahead, the possible outcomes, the possibilities are a mystery.

Then, six weeks after we switched our plans to Compton, I received a random email announcing that a prestigious foundation had named me as one of two people honored for our philanthropy. I was so certain they had the wrong Gael-Sylvia Pullen that I wrote back thanking them and letting them know they had the wrong person. The board chairman responded promptly, assuring me it wasn't an error and encouraging my attendance. The second honoree? Mayor Aja Brown of Compton.

Within the Girls Fly! Compton story are multiple amazing stories. About how Home Depot, five hundred women and girls, and others who wanted to celebrate Girls Fly! joined in. Or how Monrovia High School created six Girls Fly! Monrovia High School College Scholarships because of the excitement generated from Compton that day, the possibilities they could see. How to this day, Aja Brown and I are faith partners. There are times when I linger far too long in the mystery of disappointment that creates the "why" moments: Why did this happen this way? Why didn't I see that coming? Why didn't God respond differently? Why did it take me so long? Why did I move so quickly? Why? Why? And, in this case, why would this original plan for our national launch fall apart when everything appeared to be moving toward good outcomes? And after two years of planning. And six weeks before the event?!?

How could I trust an imperfect plan? From what I've learned so far, the gift of this new day is why it's called "the present." This is the tomorrow I spoke of yesterday. This moment is the rest of my life. This moment is what I anticipated yesterday and in yesteryears when I thought of God's promise in Jeremiah 29:11: "For I know the plans I have for you," declares the LORD, "plans to prosper you and not to harm you, plans to give you hope and a future." Even if the outcomes aren't what I hope, I have faith. That being said, how did I learn to trust an imperfect plan when my own plan had always been to speak about and believe in expectations with good outcomes, only rare moments of grief, no moments of loss, occasional moments of disappointment (if within my control), and everyday moments of peace? The answer? I had to work up to it. I had to choose to change, choose to manage my expectations, and choose to do so without becoming bitter, sarcastic, cynical, or a non-believer in the good around me.

I had to make a choice. I had to be intentional, honest, and consistent. I had to let go of my version of expected outcomes. I had to be flexible. I had to release more of my sense of control. I had to be open, patient, forgiving, and strong in my willingness to trust that good results would come from all circumstance and that though they may not always come the way I anticipated, planned for, or wanted, I could be assured that my expectations were a sign of faith, so I didn't need to be afraid.

I had to learn to have my eyes wide open to possibilities by grounding myself in daily practices of creative visualization, filling every part of my waking hours with positive input, things that would ensure hope, healing, and faith—being outdoors, listening to audiobooks or reading paperback and eBooks that reaffirm the possibilities of what I was longing for. And songs, playing songs that lift me up. Everywhere I went, everything I did, I saw an opportunity to become a better version of me, always grounding myself in the confidence and faith that Someone was bigger than I am. Because I take me wherever I go, I had to have a song that I could sing throughout the day that would give expression to my heart while replenishing my soul. That's why the "Song for the Day" became important. It's a way to cry out with joy and to express words that I couldn't find on my own. Often these words express a place deep within me that's securely anchored. Although on the surface I'm being tossed and turned, I'm intentional in my choices to be a better version of me and, for all of my imperfections, to be a part of God's perfect plan.

I encourage you to consider faith over fear. Why live small when the world of opportunities is so big? I encourage you to experience the hard-to-explain miracles that can come forth in many ways, big and small, daily or minute-by-minute. If faith is the substance of things hoped for, the evidence of things not seen, *then* fear *is false evidences appearing real. Make a choice to fill yourself with more positive than negative — more positive words, more positive people and inspirational messages that fill you with the substance of things you hope for rather than negative outcomes.*

It's my hope and prayer that you will also be the source of positive inspiration in the lives of others. May all that you fear prove to be false, and may all that you perceive as imperfect prove to be a part of God's perfect plan for your life.

I Didn't Know My Own Strength
WHITNEY HOUSTON

Yesterday
MARY MARY

RELEASING MY GRASP

"Cuidado ageno de pelo ruelga."
SPANISH

קיינער ווייס ניט וועמען דער שוך קוועטשט, נאָר דער וואָס גייט אין אים.
(Keyner veys nit vemen der shukh kvetsht, nor der vos geyt in im.)
YIDDISH

*"No one knows whose shoe pinches except
the person who walks in it."*
ENGLISH TRANSLATION

It was the early '90s, nine years after we'd packed up and moved from Los Angeles to Cleveland to launch our new business. After a long day at work, maneuvering my way home through yet another snowfall, I received a call from the night supervisor informing me that a trusted manager had stolen $25,000. It was the last straw. Gut punched, I pulled into the garage, turned off the ignition, and, tears streaming down my face, continued to listen to Mary Mary sing about having had "enough heartache" and "headache" and her determination to stop crying, get back out there, and trust God.

Since arriving in the Midwest, we'd opened multiple restaurants. Our financial journey had begun as a dream of realizing financial sufficiency, having enough so we could experience more of life in ways that we saw the world making possible for others but that seemed elusive to many we knew. Business was finally taking off, but we were exhausted from pushing, pushing, pushing to grow. I longed to be free of the striving, the struggle, the social systems we navigated to avoid isolation (the Black community in Cleveland was so different from the one we'd known in Los Angeles). Our days consisted of grinding hard work, a teeter-tottering act of work-life balance that had lasted years.

I yearned to accept who we were and where we were, to realize we'd done sufficient work, and to rest in a place of enough. But I wondered, *Will I ever get there? Will I ever recognize when enough is enough?* Three years, five years, nine years in, and I was still wondering, *Are we there yet? Isn't this the future? It kind of looks like it, but it doesn't look or feel the way I'd hoped.*

In the years since moving to Cleveland, as our lives and business had improved, two conflicting inner voices whispered to me. One voice was angelic, speaking words that uplifted me: "I'm thankful for what I have," "I'm making progress," "I'm closer than I was before." The other voice, the devil creating doubt, spoke words of defeat: "I'm working so hard and not making progress," "I'm so tired of trying to be upbeat, an inspiration to others, when *I* need inspiration," "I'm always taking two steps forward, three steps back." The voice of doubt also filled me with guilt, and that combination made me second-guess myself and suffer over the constant tough financial decisions, regurgitating phrases from a lifetime of conditioning before our newfound success: "We don't have enough for that" or "We could lose everything." For so long, we'd strived for sufficient finances, and we'd reached a place where we had more than enough, yet I was acting and speaking as if we still lacked, as through our resources weren't sufficient. My "I am" statements needed to change. The way I viewed and talked about my circumstances needed revising.

I needed to break free of the holding pattern I was in—awaiting the arrival of the future, when all promises would be fulfilled. I needed to accept the struggle, find solace in the hope offered in Jeremiah 29:11: "For I know the plans I have for you," declares the Lord, "plans to prosper you and not to harm you, plans to give you hope and a future." That winter day, sitting in the garage, I vowed to heed Mary Mary's message—to trust in God's infinite strength and abilities rather than my own limited ones. I vowed to let go, to have faith that God would make a way out of no way.

To do that, I had to look to the root of my discontent. Part of the hard-work ethic of working-class Black and Christian culture is equating hardship and resilience, philanthropy and scarcity, faith and disbelief, poverty and prosperity with being Black or White. Within the Black community, for example, we can be the nannies, the housekeepers, and the janitors, but far be it from us to *hire* a nanny, housekeeper, or maintenance worker to help us. Such help and aspirations are reserved for a rare few, who are tolerated as *exceptions*. At least this is my impression.

I love the family I grew up in, but as an adult, I'd had to flush my system of the thinking shaped by the times and culture of those days. In Cleveland, I had to take another, deeper look at how much I had incorporated those beliefs and reacted to them in others. Because such a large percentage of the African American population cultivates and exalts scarcity, I had to set boundaries and identify the lanes I belonged in, looking closely at how I chose to view faith, prosperity, and the scarcity/poverty mentality.

Up to that point, I'd had a lifetime of the poverty mentality, equating poverty with sacrificial giving to a god, to be honored only in Heaven, our eternal reward. Even today, based on the economic status of the majority of members within Black congregations, people are quick to respond negatively to "prosperity teaching." That's because many of them already have more than others and don't want the emphasis on "material things." They want to focus on the spiritual. But those struggling through hardship and rubbing two nickels together to provide for their families welcome the hope that comes from a loving, prosperous God who helps them stay encouraged through their struggles. Each group sets limits on their God beliefs. My God has no limits. That's a different perspective and often a conversation stopper.

Los Angeles is so big, so diverse, and the population so transient, that, as adults, this way of thinking wasn't in our faces day in and day out. But in the smaller community of Cleveland, it was everywhere. Neither Black nor White knew what to do with me. I wasn't like other women in the business environment of Cleveland, and I wasn't like the other Black women socially. So, I often found myself in awkward conversations as people attempted to fit our family into a particular social caste. Depending on where I showed up, in the glaring eyes of others, Black or White, I either had too little or too much. I was either Black (but not fitting the mold) or not Black enough (and not fitting in). I was succeeding in a White business environment, yet I wasn't White enough because I lacked a corporate culture education.

Being an outcast because of where we lived or worked was a new experience for us. No matter how I tried, I was never enough. Something had to give. While living in Japan, I'd learned that there's something inherently valuable about being a misfit. Not that every person who steps outside social and economic stereotypes must be a social outcast, but there's definitely value in identifying yourself differently and eventually owning it with a smile.

I'd been waiting for years for permission to be released from the social pressures of the Cleveland caste system, pressures resulting from our rising economic status. But I'd had enough of waiting, so I decided to give *myself* permission to let go of the old mentality. To get to a place of igniting a sense of faith, I would have to give birth to a new perspective.

I prayed into my desires to change the trajectory of our family history and find the words to redefine our experiences. I searched the scriptures, read self-help, inspirational, and spiritual books, devoured audio tapes and sermons, and practiced motivational messages and visualization exercises as I prayed for words to be spoken into me. I also longed to change the trajectory of future generations. My hunger to rise above this restrictive belief system became a calling to pour possibility, openness, and joy into the lives of our son, our employees, and our community.

To break the ingrained myths and hidden stories resulting from unexamined beliefs that I had previously told myself, I had to take two major steps.

STEP 1. I would have to stay diligent in keeping my outlook positive—using positive words, seeking out positive surroundings, and finding the lessons and joy in experiences. I had to continuously repair the holes where hope leaked out, draining my energy. It worked to my advantage that I had years of visualization practice to support this shift in my subconscious. I also had more than thirty years of regular physical training to support my mental focus, but this didn't mean that my muscles didn't weaken during periods of inactivity. It did mean, however, for my mind, body, and soul, a deeply encrypted neurological and muscle memory would kick-start me back to recovery faster and stronger, regardless of the number of setbacks I experienced. As long as I kept moving in the direction of expectation, I felt as if the entire universe was aligned to make it my reality.

STEP 2. I would have to start within my own household. I had learned something important about my role of wife and mother early in the childrearing ages: It was my responsibility to influence the rhythm and atmosphere within our home. If we were to have memories of peace, joy, and laughter, I had to be a happy mother. I had to be this person *for myself* and not wait for others to determine who and how I should be at each moment. Each moment was well within my grasp, and it had to begin with my internal attitude. I would be responsible for listening, trusting, and obeying this longing calling out to me. It truly didn't matter if my cup was half full or half empty. I could always refill from a larger-than-life pitcher of possibilities. I set out to make every space around me a conscious reflection of my inner world, my state of mind, soul, and being. I would embrace the magnificent mysteries of life.

As an adult, the more I had explored outside the boundaries of my community—the more I traveled, interacted in the world of business, and met more diverse people—the more I saw how abundant and rich life was, and how vast the possibilities. Because of that, I sought new ways of expressing myself, and a new language began to form. Now that I'd landed in Cleveland, my expansion of thinking and redefinition of myself continued. No longer did I say things like "That's not possible. We can't afford it." Instead, I became known for saying, "Don't tell me what we can't do. Show and tell me the options for what we can do."

Not only was I developing a new language of opportunity and possibility as my different worlds converged, a new me was evolving too. My old world in Los Angeles county had prepared me to take a community lead during a potential racial clash between Korean merchants and Black consumers. I had lived through racial clashes before—the Watt's Riots in 1965, the LA riots in 1992—which made it easy to recognize the warning signs and engage people in unexpected ways. And my years of success in the White male-dominated field of commercial real estate, along with extensive experience from living abroad, prepared me to handle complex situations. I began to see that my difference was valuable, and I looked for ways to appreciate who I was and trust where we were going. I decided to have fun on my new path to learning too.

It was a relief just being me and not trying to impress anybody. When people in our expanding social circle asked what we did for a living (how we found ourselves among their ranks), I no longer pretended that they might actually be interested in getting to know me. I quickly ended all speculation (as did Mark), and saved a lot of time and energy, by saying, "We cook hamburgers." The authenticity of their character would rise like oil in water. Most people were too slow to keep their gut reaction from showing on their faces. It was such a relief to just do me, to be comfortable with who I was, and pray to God that there were good people who would embrace the goodness of our hearts.

The judgment came from both sides. For one event we hosted, I commissioned a troupe of twenty African dancers to perform a dance traditionally associated with the celebrations of birth, progress, provision, and blessing. For years we'd brought in this troupe for the community during Black History Month celebrations and at schools, to expand their educational arts experiences.

The difference this time—the performance was at our home. Jubilant singing and dancing filled the house. I rejoiced. As I danced among our guests, checking to see if anyone needed anything, I overheard two uninvited friends of the troupe talking about Mark and me. "The bougie Black people think they're better than everyone else," one of them said, and the other agreed.

I was stunned. Being called bougie and in our own home! No! I was through with the sting of other's judgments. I turned around and promptly showed those two the door. The words in that single sentence of judgment caused a major shift in my mindset, forcing me daily to examine the details of sufficiency associated with what defines my contentment, my appreciation for joy and beauty. I stopped assuming everyone would understand me and that they, too, must see the good around us. I stopped assuming that what brought me peace of mind and beauty was tangible and evident to everyone. During the course of ordinary moments this simple question, *Am I sharing to much of myself with others who may not welcome or understand me?* required me to rethink and further release my own expectations of others to experience contentment, and more frequent moments of peace, joy, and laughter.

"My much may be too much for someone else," Pastor T.D. Jakes says in a podcast. After that winter day in our garage, my "how much is enough" shifted from calculating our tangible assets and weighing social acceptance to "How much is enough for *me, defined by God's greatness and not others?*" The mornings started with, "Have I had enough sleep for the intense exercise and training I'm about enjoy at 5:30 a.m.?" "Have I eaten enough food to fuel my activity?" "Have I spent enough time in quiet to enter the battlefield of challenges coming at the office on my schedule today?"

I had to pay closer attention to who I was talking to and who was speaking into me. I had to identify the moments, the people, each circumstance, and the voices within and without that created myths of lack and scarcity, prosperity, and the size of the eye of the needle that I would have to walk through. The seeds they planted had deep roots infiltrating almost every aspect of my life: the neighborhoods I believed I could live in; the community organizations I had not considered joining; places I was nervous about visiting, but ventured into despite the trepidation; my level of business and global community engagement. Although the conversations were laced with faith, hope, and love, for the most part, everything had always been spoken from a place of not having enough, making it appear to be almost impossible to get to a place of *enoughness*. Every meeting, every conversation, every decision had been creating a deficient relationship within myself—the "siren song of the consumer culture" author Lynn Twist calls it.

This was the head on the nail piercing my financial soul: *I lack sufficient knowledge and experience* to know how to take what I have and make this more than enough. Unwittingly, I had given myself permission to stay in a mental place of lack and allow myself to be applauded for it—and frowned upon when I had too much. When I exceeded the expectations of others, making them uncomfortable with themselves, I would pull back. With too much education, I was called high-falutin' in some circles. Without education enough, I was an Affirmative Action Quota. If, when speaking to parents of our son's schoolmates, I talked of travels to the distant lands when they considered Disney World a stretch, I would rephrase the experience to make it sound like an aspiration instead of a past experience. This type of mental gymnastics drains us of our faith in God, our joy for life, and I had had enough of trying. I decided to switch lanes, change my language even more, and expand my circle of friends.

Staying true to the core values of who I am and who I am thankful to be—myself, a daughter of the Great Creator of the universe and no one else—during our remaining years in Cleveland was not always easy. I drew strength from a visit I made to Soweto, South Africa, four years after arriving in Cleveland. Amidst the extreme poverty, there was singing, smiling, laughing, hugging, and the wide-open arms of people who looked like me, saying, "Welcome home my sister. Welcome home!" That community gave me a resting place for my soul, a place to feel welcomed and at home, and that welcome had nothing to do with the amount of resources any of us had. It was the love and acknowledgement of one human being to another that was rich and satisfying. Feeling welcomed by them was an experience beyond my wildest dreams, and I carried that feeling home with me to Cleveland.

As the years passed in Cleveland and after, my faith was ignited and my language altered again and again by experiences I couldn't have imagined. When I visited the White House twice within one year: once as a first-time board member of a Korean Christian community development agency to attend a Christian-Asian White House summit; and once as a guest of the White House education staff because of my philanthropy and community work for Girls Fly! When we brought our Girls Fly! philanthropy model to the First Lady of Belize. And when we heard our son's voice calling from Oxford College one summer, after spending the previous summer at Stanford while he was still in high school. These experiences were exciting, but it was my deep, unending gratitude that consistently fed my feeling of contentment. Nothing felt excessive or insufficient in those conscious moments of thanks. The experiences and feelings felt like familiar necessities, simply equipping us to handle more, while sitting comfortably with what we had.

Those twelve years in Cleveland, the question *When is enough enough?* kept showing up in my thoughts, and my response echoed in my words to our family: "I am truly thankful for everything, every experience, and the joy of being content, whether we have much or little." I knew I was heading in the right direction when I heard my husband and son join in: "I know! So am I."

I encourage you to look closer at how much you, too, are blessed. You can choose to gaze in despair at the scarcity or insufficiency of your circumstances, or you can take a breath and brave your deepest fears. Even if you've never thought of yourself as a religious person, you're still a person of faith. You had faith that you'd wake up this morning, that you'd breathe, that you'd get to places you planned to reach and back, despite the odds of interruption. Explore expanding your faith experiences by looking around you at all that's in front of you. Make faith observations—something that makes you smile that you've never noticed or acknowledged, such as daffodils in your neighbor's yard, a stranger smiling "Good morning!," bread. Anything! And guard your heart, mind, and home from those who can't celebrate the wonder of life with you.

It's my hope and prayer that these details of gratitude will fuel your faith, along with listening to how others overcame similar challenges. Gather all the resources you can to fill your cup of joy, and may it run over.

What Is This?
BISHOP EDWIN HAWKINS

Defying Gravity
IDINA MENZEL

CRAZY FAITH

"Hatari kubwa kwa wengi wetu sio kuwa lengo letu ni ya juu sana na hatuwezi kulifikia mbali ni la chini sana na tunalifikia."

"The greatest danger for most of us is not that our aim is too high and we miss it, but that is it too low and we reach it."

**ATTRIBUTED TO MICHELANGELO,
SWAHILI AND ENGLISH VERSIONS**

I t was January 2019, and we'd entered the new year with peace, hope, and hard work. Life had been refilled with new memories of laughter, youthful voices of all ages, and high hopes for a new season. California was experiencing an outpouring of rain after years of drought and we were among the many anticipating robust blessings. Eighteen days into the new year, news came of the first of many unexpected deaths, Uncle Harold, the life of the party we only seemed to see at funerals. We were on a flight from Detroit to Greensboro, North Carolina, to attend his funeral, when we hit an extremely rough patch. Fear and faith battled for a place in my thoughts. I was reading Francis Chan's book, *Crazy Faith*. The more I read about stepping into the unknown and trusting that good can come from it, the more turbulent the external conditions around us became.

As a passenger, I had no control. The plane rose and dropped, shimmied and shook. We hadn't paid or signed up to experience this bumpy scary ride to reach our destination. I wanted smooth sailing. I wanted to read about crazy faith, not experience the unexpected turbulence sometimes required to get from one place to another. Thoughts of a recent plane crash in England filled my head with visuals of grieving families. I searched frantically to recall images that would recalibrate my fears.

Like a dog scratching desperately in the dirt under a rose bush or a cartoon of a character tossing clothing, shoes, and lost trinkets from under the bed into the air, searching frantically for some item he or she was desperate to find, I searched through my thoughts for something of great value that I needed within this moment. Peace. I needed peace. I needed peace from fear. I needed peace as an act of nature outside this plane! Reading about faith in the face of fear became a struggle. I was scared! Really scared.

Ten years earlier, we'd been in a similar situation on a flight from Cleveland to Arizona. We'd flown to Cleveland in January for the funeral of our dear, dear friend and business colleague Jim Senior. We'd moved from the Cleveland area and were still settling into a new life in Tucson. Although we had a home and real estate in Ohio, it was the investments in friendships that meant the most to us. Many of these friendships carried us through the harsh realities of feeling alone in an environment that could sometimes feel as cold and perplexing as a Northeast winter. The warmth of these friendships ran deep, many becoming extended family during the two decades of living so far away from our blood family.

We received the call about Jim Senior ten days after we'd received a similar call about his thirty-eight-year-old son, Jim Junior, who had died tragically. That call came during the funeral dinner in Connecticut, when we were still in the depths of mourning our own beloved Aunt Puddy. Jim Senior's was a graveside funeral, and the exceptionally cold weather had Mark and me trying to warm our bodies and console ourselves for our triple loss. After the funeral, we drove directly to Cleveland's Hopkins airport, where I waited inside the warm terminal while Mark returned the rental car before we boarded our flight for Tucson. In our grief, we found a way to laugh at how crazy it was to have lived through many a freezing cold Cleveland winter. He dropped me off smiling (we'd been joking about the cold—we used to say "It's stupid cold out," when we lived there), but something happened within the fewer than fifteen minutes he'd been gone, because when he arrived from dropping off the rental car, he was no longer smiling, but sad again, wearing the same expression he'd worn that morning. He didn't say a word as we cleared TSA, just held my hand tighter, looked at me, and then looked away, saying, "I love you, Babe."

My heart broke for the spouses of those who'd passed, and for the fact that their deaths were leaving broken hearts, two from marriages older than ours. They also left young adult grieving children, nieces, nephews, parents (in Jim Jr.'s case), friends, neighbors, and colleagues — all missing them. It wasn't until we buckled our seat belts and heard the flight attendant make some reference to putting on our own oxygen masks before trying to help others and that we could find the emergency instructions and exits in front of us, that Mark's squeeze of my hand prompted me to stare straight into his eyes. Before takeoff, he gave me the news of another death, that of our vibrant, beloved thirty-five-year-old niece Misti. There's no perfect time for unexpected death. Misti's, too, was an untimely loss, and we were going to have to hold on tightly to each other to make it through the next journey. My own words felt eerily soft.

I watched Mark's lips move but I couldn't hear or see anything clearly through my tears. The flight home that day was deadly silent. No words of comfort could mend or replace the fractured part of our broken hearts.

That flight across country of ten years prior carried frightened passengers through extremely tumultuous weather. The plane rose and fell, rocked and shook with a fierceness determined to scare us to death. We were tired, extremely tired. Sheer exhaustion had already tapped into the last reserves of my hope, and we were much too exhausted to be afraid any longer of death.

And here we were again, 2019, flying to another unexpected funeral in turbulent conditions. Grief and fear were tossing me around. I couldn't pretend that the cabin wasn't eerily silent, indicating that I wasn't the only one afraid. I couldn't do a thing about any of it. Then I was reminded to speak the words that Christ spoke to the storm: "Peace. Be still." (Mark 4:39) Exhaustion required the sweet peace of sleep and rest. Momentarily or eternally, it didn't matter. I had spoken these words of Christ many times before and have spoken them many times since. Each time, calm returned. On this flight, however, fear continued. I was confused. What had worked before wasn't working now. I couldn't help myself. I was scared. Suppressing my fear became impossible and my manicured nails clenching my husband's leg would later reveal five odd bruises on his thigh. I put my book down. I closed my eyes. I looked away from the window and into my husband's shoulder and said, "Lord, I'm still trusting you, and I'm still scared. I'm reading and speaking Your word and about how awesome You are, and I'm still scared."

Unable to pretend, to deny the truth of the circumstances, I cried out: "Let them know we love them (if this plane goes down while I'm squeezing Mark's leg). Let them know You love them."

I braced myself for the worst and rested in the fact that regardless of the turbulence, everything would be okay. My clouded thoughts have always eventually cleared. Not always when I want, but perfectly timed. The storms always passed. "You still love us and Your love will last." That's all I could say and do. Nothing else was in my control.

I can't help but wonder if the sincerity of my faith, even in fearful moments, didn't bring a smile to the face of God? It seems that I used the words of my heart not to describe the situation but to change it. As soon as I relaxed, the storm calmed. It wasn't until then that I recalled a story I'd heard about a young boy on a plane, playing with his toy on his tray table while everyone else was gasping and clenching with fear during a very turbulent flight. The flight attendants had taken their seats, a sure sign that these were not idyllic flying conditions. Despite the fear surrounding him, the little boy played with child-like glee. "Aren't you scared?" his seatmate asked him. The little boy kept playing, no eye contact, but responded, "No. Why should I be? My father's the pilot."

I encourage you to ponder whom and what you have sincere faith in. You may not consider yourself a religious person, but if you leave your home today, you have faith that you'll return. If you get in a car, on a train or bus, you have faith you'll reach your destination.

It's my hope and prayer that you will have faith that something good is trying to find a place within your life today. Look for it. Snap a photo of it. You'll know you're seeing with fresh eyes because it will make you smile, and that's a sign that the storm is calming down.

Sing a Simple Song

SLY & THE FAMILY STONE

LAUGH OUT LOUD

"At the height of laughter, the universe is flung into a kaleidoscope of new possibilities."

JEAN HOUSTON

I was in need of more laughter. Real, deep, childlike, side-aching laughter. The sun was up, our bedroom door cracked open. I lay under the covers, listening to our almost two-year-old niece in the next room, singing to herself and laughing alone. Until I heard her, I hadn't realized how long it had been since I'd fallen over laughing so hard that I had to get up and run to the restroom.

I was less curious about what was causing her to laugh than I was about why I never caught myself singing and laughing anymore when I was alone or when I *felt* alone. The burdens of adulthood and the myriad of responsibilities that come with life had muted my heart's song. Especially recently. The problems with my heart were persistent from myocarditis and other inexplicable medical complications—evidence of years of life stresses. The loss of health, loss of business, income, relationships and, yes, even lives, had taken its toll. I was in month five of what would turn out to be a fifteen-month journey of being severely restricted physically, often bedridden.

Hearing my niece singing and laughing made me want to sing and laugh out loud again. But where to begin? How did I get to a place where laughter and song felt natural again? Years of my life had already been devoted to minute-by-minute commitments to look for the good around me and to be fueled by the goodness of life. Yet still, here I lay in a tumble of blankets sorting through the tangled emotions of a jacked-up life. Within my mind and broken heart were unsung songs I had to wrestle to the surface. Still my niece sang. Despite her being born into an emotionally volatile home, a home so stressful when she was an infant that I'd worried that the stress would rob her of her childhood, her ability for joy, I discovered my niece always woke up this way—singing, laughing, content. She'd come to stay with us for a while, until things straightened out at home. Unaware of the circumstances that had temporarily landed her in our home that autumn morning, this sweet little girl with her sagging diaper encouraged me to get up.

So how could I get back to that place where I sang and laughed out loud? Two quotes collided in my mind as I searched for an answer. "It's never too late to have a happy childhood" by the author Tom Robbins. And the fashion icon Coco Chanel's famous observation: "Nature gives you the face you have at 20. Life shapes the face you have at 30. But at 50, you get the face you deserve." I wanted a face that radiated with joy! I wanted a heart that was healed and allowed my body to move with the joy of riding my bike long distances again, compete in ballroom dance competitions again, roller blade along the beach paths, all things I had anticipated doing when we moved to California. I wanted the longings of the little girl inside me to get up and sing and laugh with this little girl in the other room. The joy of both little girls seemed worth holding on to. When I was fifty, people thought I was thirty-five. Now, just a few years later, I doubted anyone would shave fifteen years off my age.

I'd always taken care of myself. I'd reaped the rewards of eating right, fueling the level of activity I enjoyed. In fact, even during my relatively temporary moment of sickness, the doctors and nurses marveled that I was still alive and attributed it to my lifestyle. For someone as active, vibrant, and intentionally consciousness of filling every space in our home and in my life with peace, joy, and laughter, someone who for fifty years ate, slept, and lived the most balanced life possible, this health crisis was hard to understand. It felt like the equivalent of being given a diagnosis of lung cancer when I'd never smoked. (Even that thought reminds me to be thankful—I don't have lung cancer.) But I would be well again. I wanted my happy childhood back!

In that moment, I decided it wasn't too late to begin again. I would treat my life like it was a work of art, ever evolving, one that held multiple opportunities for me to recreate myself. While I might not stop revisiting the facts of my life—the good, the bad, the painful, and the joyful—I would revisit them with a fresh perspective of adventure. I would allow the ordinary to become extraordinary and hope that along the way I would find my voice, a singing voice. Life is a trip! No, seriously. Life is a trip with a capital "T" *and* a lowercase "t." It can be both a crazy wild scary ride one minute and a smooth sailing routine the next *and* a journey that we take one step at a time, one foot in front of the other.

From that point forward, I vowed that when I revisited my own personal narrative, I would watch as the events of my life transformed into "the kaleidoscope of new possibilities" Jean

Houston references. It's true. Living a life filled with laughter and golden adventures is a gentle process of choosing to root out the negative and plant the good. It's a decision, a moment-to-moment decision. I'm guided by this philosophy with each choice I make. Once again, within the sweet blessed gift of that moment, I found myself gently moved toward optimism. It's not like joy comes and stays in the same spot day after day. It's often elusive, yet ever present. I have to look for joy and seize every opportunity to ensure its presence in daily circumstances. Unlike happiness, I find that joy is a more stable sense of well-being, one not dictated solely by how others make me feel, but by the state of mind I choose to experience.

My first Picture of the Day, eleven years earlier, was a card with two senior year ladies sitting in a crowd. They looked like sisters. But the strong resemblance was questionable because they wore their sun-wrinkled faces so differently. One had an irritable, sour expression etched into her weary forehead. Perhaps you've noticed the deep lines that find a home in the face of grumpy people who are bitter and hardened from life's experiences. The tightness around their mouths that form because they don't smile, the suspicious and unapproachable look in their eyes. It was hard to imagine any kind words coming from her tight lips.

On the other hand, the woman next to her, having apparently grown up in the same environment, was glowing. Her eyes twinkled, and it wasn't a Photoshopped image. No make-up. The lines of time had created a beauty that clearly reflected a calm, joyful temperament. A mindset. A choice. I wanted to be reminded daily to move toward optimism, to carve joy into the spirit of my disposition. Our family has an expression: "If you don't start nothing, there won't be nothing." To me it means, if I don't start a bad behavior, I don't have to worry about kicking a bad behavior. And on the flip side, if I start a good behavior, I'll have a good behavior in place.

It's a constant choice.

With my two-year-old niece singing in the next room, I recalled the sounds of singing and the sound of laughter from another niece, our thirty-five-year-old niece Misti, who'd died a couple of years earlier. Such a tragic loss. She was the life of every party. The Saturday morning she died began as many other Saturdays had, with her two sons, Marquex, a senior in high school, and Michael, in middle school, at home. That morning, Misti sat at her computer preparing the annual school excursion to Washington, D.C., adding all her signature elements to ensure joy and laughter on that history field trip. When Marquex heard his happy-go-lucky mother yelling his name, he rushed to the living room only to find that she'd already called 911 due to having trouble breathing. Within minutes she died. Heart attack? Deep vein thrombosis? Whatever it was, she was gone.

Among the many lessons I learned during that time of mourning was the unexpected response of the funeral director when I commented on how natural Misti looked lying in state at the funeral home. "Oh, it was an honor to be with her," he said, and then proceeded to describe her personality in ways that only people close to her would know.

Puzzled, I asked, "When did you meet Misti?"

"Oh. I didn't know her when she was alive," he said. "What people don't realize is that there's a muscle memory, and that memory stays intact when we pass. We have the loved ones of the deceased wanting us to make their family member look happier or more relaxed or kinder. But we can't do that once they've died. We do the best we can, but some things are only within their control while living."

My husband, brother, sister-in-law, and I teared up, but those tears were different from those we'd been shedding. These were tears of joy and gratitude. Misti had lived a joy-filled life. Part genetic, mostly choice. Even in her passing, she brought us joy in a way that was beyond skin deep. We were deeply moved. We had never before experienced wisdom and insights on how to live our lives through the eyes of someone who worked with the dead.

That morning, listening to my niece singing in the bathroom, I added to my practice of choosing a Song of the Day. I decided to include a Song of the Week and a Song of the Year, one I hum and carry with me throughout each day—my personal buoy to cling to, to stay afloat when the sinking moments of life try to pull me under. As I write this, that little girl in the next room is now eight-years-old. She still sings to herself and laughs out loud. There are five more little ones now, her cousins, who spend time with us, and they do the same. Fortunately for me, they're learning new songs from me, moment by moment, and a dance to go along with them.

I encourage you to be intentional about smiling and laughing more. In her blog post "How to Laugh More—22 Ways to Bring More Laughter into Your Life," attorney and entrepreneur Marelisa Fabrege writes, "When you smile, happy changes begin to take place automatically, both internally and externally. In addition, you can think of smiling as a warmup for laughing." Why not make smiling a goal?

I set goals in all areas that I desire to see progress toward a desired outcome, and sometimes within a desired time frame. I set goals when I exercise. I've made it a goal to connect with people I enjoy being with. A lifetime goal of mine is to be known for my joyful spirit, my optimistic, inspirational disposition; although it doesn't come easily or as naturally as I may desire. For this reason, I'm encouraging you, too, to be intentional about setting a goal to laugh more. Remind yourself as part of your morning and evening routine. I started this practice with a desktop calendar filled with a joke for the day. It helped me not to take everything too seriously.

It's my hope and prayer that you have fun. Go on a field trip. Go! Go visit one place that you have been driving by. Perhaps it is a nursery, coffee shop, museum, theater, school. Whatever it is, go off your beaten path and start moving in a new direction. And turn the music up! Sing along! Sing out loud. If you must, start by humming the tune. You will be met with more joy, more singing out loud, and more laughter. The more often you go with these practices, the more you will refill the empty places in your life that were void of joy and laughter. What better time to start than now? As for me, I'm going kayaking.

What Shall I Do

1990 REV. JAMES CLEVELAND AND
THE SOUTHERN CALIFORNIA COMMUNITY CHOIR

STARTING ON
A FAITH JOURNEY

*"We may have all come on different ships,
but we're in the same boat."*

REV. DR. MARTIN LUTHER KING, JR.

Many people choose to begin a spiritual journey to be closer to God and to have the value and purpose of their life confirmed. Others embark on a spiritual journey when life-altering decisions must be made and they feel too small to carry the burden of big life changes. And some take this journey because of the impact of unexpected changes in circumstances that leave them feeling lost, hurt, and confused. The raw force of a crisis can sting, leaving us vulnerable and open to the toxic opinions of others. Unless we take steps to seek spiritual answers apart from the noises bombarding us externally, we miss the power and presence of what's being whispered internally.

Americans tend to be negligent in our spiritual understanding, and what understanding we do have decreases as media, scientific, and alternative resources jockey for our attention. We tend to neglect our spiritual makeup, focusing more on logic, mindfulness, and physical activities in the pursuit of explanations. Spiritual journeys allow us to reconnect with more of who we are, expand our awareness, gain a different perspective on our problems. They free us to confidently redefine what success means to us, see a greater purpose for our life, and understand how to come to peace with the world. The purpose of a spiritual journey is bigger than finding an answer; it's a process of continually asking questions.

So how do you begin? Start where you are and take one step at a time. I'm learning that seeking answers to all my questions doesn't have to mean I'm paralyzed or doubting my faith in God. When I cultivate hope in my life, I don't become immobilized by seemingly insurmountable problems. Instead, I look for concrete opportunities to engage and take a step of faith, using joy as my barometer, one step at a time, minute by minute. The minutes become hours, and before I know it a day, a week, a month has transitioned me from a place of despair to a place of peace, joy, and laughter. My hope is wrapped within my faith.

"Now faith is confidence in what we hope for and assurance about what we do not see." (Hebrews 11:1). Hope is an optimistic attitude of mind based on an expectation of positive outcomes. Faith says that a positive outcome is already here. Hope says that a positive outcome could happen in the future. So stay strong, hold on.

We need faith to connect the power of our perceptions as human beings to the spiritual realm, which links us to God and makes Him a tangible reality. We need faith for increased awareness and to experience possibilities greater than we could on our own. Faith is the basic ingredient needed to begin a relationship with God. Faith in its ultimate meaning is an unshakable inner belief that all things are indeed working together for good and that good will prevail and its evidence will be tangible. A big factor of faith is recognizing that we have no control, that there's a greater power, and that we need to stay firmly grounded in this attitude of hope.

I can't always explain it, but I know Who and what I know to be true. I know Who and what I know can bring forth good as promised and hoped for. Just as I can't see air but know it exists and gives me life. I can't see electricity, but it's there—lighting, heating, and suppling power to our homes. Other men and women have had access to the same resources, but harnessing the unseen is the work of minds and hearts that isolate themselves from the narrow beliefs of others. In the case of electricity that someone (or those throughout the ages who contributed to its discovery) had enough faith and belief in the power of the unknown to exist that I can write now in the light of that truth and through a variety of light sources. Thank you, Benjamin Franklin, for your work with electricity. Thank you, Thomas Edison, for the light bulb. Thank you, God!

Part of my faith journey, specifically with Girls Fly!, has been the many moments of doing grunt work in the face of uncertainty (also known as fear of failure), laboring alone, constantly explaining to others what feels obvious to me, moving the wheels forward and not arriving, yet arriving. I'm still on the Girls Fly! journey, and its unfolding has been amazing—partnering with top brands and expanding around the globe. When I think about the faithfulness of Noah building the ark before the great flood, I sigh. I stop my internal grumbling, get up, and carry on. Like Noah, I have added a massive undertaking to all my daily responsibilities, in my case, launching a global project and writing a book.

Noah probably rose early and worked late gathering and preparing the wood, one more chore toward fulfilling a vison pursued with faith and in hope. The timing for both of us was clearly not based on logical business plans and weather conditions.

He was building a water vessel sitting in the heat of a dry desert. He had no support. At the time of launching Girls Fly!, I was sitting in the Tucson desert preparing to close up business there, letting go of all the human and financial resources that would have made a launch of this magnitude well-supported.

Within months, I would be back home in Southern California, at the water's edge, to set sail with Girls Fly!, a vast fleet of metaphorical ships ready to forge uncharted waters. While my vision was clear, my ability to move forward had been limited. Doing the impossible only becomes clearer once it's accomplished. Everyone can then see and believe. Like Noah, I had to keep moving forward toward an intense internal calling when no one else could hear or see what we were doing. I'm certain it was an internal North Star guiding us forward. To receive a vision so clear to him, spoken into his heart, without anyone seeing that same vision or hearing those same words in their hearts, must have been perplexing for Noah. I try to imagine Noah's thoughts.

He was a man like men today. He surely questioned. He surely had moments of doubt played out in his self-talk, and apparently God didn't have a problem with that. He understood. But when the added pressure of other people's doubts is tossed into our own pile of questions, life can feel out of balance. I can't help but wonder if Noah's conversations were in a louder or barely audible voice when he was talking to God? Or were the opinions of others and their dissatisfaction an irritation? Certainly there were mumblings circulating: "Who does he think he is to hear from the Creator of the Universe and not us?"

Internal and external mutterings can wear us down and carve away at our faith and leave us hopeless. Not so with Noah. I, too, shall finish my task to reach one million women and girls with a message of hope and inspiration, to reaffirm the value of their most cherished and sacred dreams, to create a replicable philanthropic program and investment model that is self-sustaining. For this reason, I kept seeking what Noah had, in order to finish the enormous task placed in his care. I imagine he limited his exposure to those asking negative questions, limited the frequency of his own. I wonder how he stayed tuned into the calling that was given to him within the circumstances? He stayed intentional in his faith and grounded in his hope. I'm convinced God put a song in his heart, and he quickly assembled the materials on hand and jimmy-rigged a way to carve grooves into the stories of his faith with each repeated sound of the hammer nailing that ark together, the song of his tools creating notes that embodied what's required in life. That song repeated over and over again, as a complete symphonic melody as a lead solo. He had to have hummed a song.

I'm convinced that faith is a blend of conscious choice within each moment, asking for divine intervention, and the intentional pursuit of having a dream come true. Although Mark and I had dreamed of moving closer to home after years in Ohio, and because of the heat of the economic crisis we faced in the summer heat of Arizona, we found ourselves no closer to the water than Noah was when he built the ark. We had relocated based on a dream. Even though it had become a nightmare as we struggled to hold on to our faith, we couldn't control how much life tossed us. We had entered what we didn't realize would become an extended journey. Instead of unending rain, we would experience something closer to a drought. Yet it was the calling and the vision that was put on my heart for Girls Fly! A vision that just wouldn't go away, and that got us into this messy and stormy period. How nice it would have been to have reaffirming voices saying, "No, you've got it right. Keep going. Keep going!"

No voices came. No surprise knocks at the door from anyone who just happened to be in the area and had been thinking of us. The only reminders of people heading in directions unknown and reaching some version of a promised land filled with milk and honey were those I found in God's Word, the Bible. Of course, I devoured self-help and inspirational books. Most of them pointed back to the wisdom of the Word and stories of others who had also been caught in extreme circumstances. I couldn't read them. I wanted to close my mind to the path of self-questioning they could open, questions such as, "If you think this is bad, things could be worse" and then have them get worse. I needed and wanted to close off all fear while keeping a small opening for good to find its way in and water the mustard seed-sized faith.

Sometimes, there are moments where it is just the Lord and me. Fortunately for me, Mark gets that and understands. But again, doing something with the magnitude of Girls Fly! was daunting—when Mark and I had business responsibilities that included at the top of the list considering employees and their families, community commitments, influence, status, access, a voice; when more dreams were spiraling out of control as the economy sank, the murders at the border were increasing, and our isolation and despair went unsupported and without answers. We had responsibilities. We had shelter, income, and obligations. We had a desire for financial freedom, but at what price? We didn't have time to dream altruistic dreams of inspiring others to see the good around us. At least, that's how I felt.

There are times in life when the only solution is the best solution: to walk, sing, and pray, to look for all the good around us. For Mark and me, it wasn't easy to do that when tripping in the darkness of the unknown, when life as we'd known it for twenty years was being ripped away. Solitude provides answers that are often missed in the busyness of life. In my solitude I was able to hear the voice of God speak directly to my feelings, our circumstances and doubts. Through songs, random quotes that would pop-up on my computer, sermons, podcasts, and relaxation visualization practice, I became more thankful for both Mark's and God's re-affirming words to "Keep going. We'll figure it out together, just keep going."

One day, after we had left Arizona for California, I'd been hammering away at getting Girls Fly! off the ground for hours. It didn't feel like there was any sign of sustainable financial change for us, yet I continued pursuing the calling of Girls Fly! while multitasking income-producing real estate jobs in a bad economy—all from a wheelchair. Although the pressures we experienced in Arizona eventually got us closer to water and home, a big change still hadn't taken place. I was hopeful of regaining health and financial stability, and realizing the dream of Girls Fly! to reach others.

How could faith and hope be stressful? I thought about the beauty around me. We were no longer in the physical surroundings of a dry desert, yet the isolation of my dream regarding Girls Fly! continued. During a moment of weariness, I cried out to God through more tears. I had been sitting on the side of the bed before dropping to my knees asking, "What shall I do, Lord? What steps shall I take? Oh, Lord, what shall I do?" I was singing my prayer. I thought about Noah, how he must have had moments of doubting what he'd seen and heard. I wanted to be sure that I'd heard Him right. *Maybe...maybe I'd gotten it wrong? Maybe the vision of what I'd been seeing all this time was incorrect.* Earlier that day, I'd been on a conference call with two skeptical people. The seeds of their doubt were trying to find a place to bury themselves in my mind. For a second, a split second, I pondered if they were right and I was wrong. Then, as soon as the question crossed my mind, a reaffirming message from the Lord came saying, "Don't be discouraged. Don't wallow in fear. It is disguised as discouragement."

I was also reminded of the many long-distance drives Mark and I had taken in unfamiliar territory during the pre-GPS era, the times we felt we'd veered off course or found ourselves lost. Help came in the form of a road map provided by AAA or a local Thomas Guide. As long as we kept moving in the direction that someone else had laid out, we would reach our desired destination, and right on time. Today, in this era of the automated voices, we never hear these intangible sources saying, "You're doing well. Keep going. You're on the right path, heading in the right direction." But we choose to listen to our inner voice and keep moving in the direction we were destined for.

I pulled myself off the floor and kneeled beside our bed, feeling trapped within the prison of my own fears, crying, praying through the thick cloud of uncertainty and doubt. Then my cellphone rang. At first, I wasn't going to answer, but at the last minute, I reached for the phone. Out of the blue, a voice from seemingly nowhere called me by name.

"Hey Gael-Sylvia," she said.

It was Christine, a woman who'd worked with Nelson Mandela. Those all-world birthday parties they had for him? She coordinated those. I hadn't talked to her in a couple of years. "You've been on my mind. I just feel like I know you're trying to raise the money so that you can hire me, but I feel like I should just start working with you. I should help you keep this moving so you don't give up."

I hadn't talked to this woman in years! We'd never met face to face. We'd only talked on the phone. Just the timing of her call was sufficient to keep me going. Perhaps it was her global experiences working with President Mandela, but in an instant, I was reminded of something I once read that Nelson Mandela said: "The brave man is not he who does not feel afraid, but he who conquers that fear." Our fears of failure, judgement, and disappointment can make it hard to be brave. My battle with unfounded fears of feeling foolish if my faith-based actions didn't produce the intended outcomes was a huge internal mountain that I had to face.

Mountain climbing requires active protection, aid, and an anchor. Although conquering mountains of fear sometimes feels like it requires a willpower and an internal strength that I don't always have, in those moments I also experience what the Lord said to Paul: "My grace is sufficient for you, for my power is made perfect in weakness." (2 Corinthians: 12:9) Dreamers and visionaries may look foolish to others, but as Paul said to the Corinthians, "I have made a fool of myself, but you drove me to it." We become weary, fearful, and discouraged in the loneliness of a dream journey not because of the task, but because so few people experience the power of fully living beyond themselves. There would be no need for the word "miracle" if living miraculous lives was the norm.

Living and leading from a place of joy is similar to a long-distance relay race. Sometimes people come along beside us for a specific task, within a specific moment, and for a very specific purpose. They are a part of our relay team. But I view myself as the captain of my life, and although others may drop in and out of this race toward my dreams, I must always keep going toward the goal. I have a tendency to want to stay with everybody forever and ever and ever! It did eventually become clear that Christine's role at that time was for that specific moment only. The encouragement she provided was sufficient to keep me going. She handed me the baton of encouragement to keep running the race set before me. Hopefully, sometime in the future, we'll reconnect, but that moment wasn't about my connection with her. It was about the Lord lifting me up from a moment of discouragement to say, "No, you're on the right track, keep going and I'm with you, you're not alone." In His solitude, how many conversations did Noah have with God that lifted him above the chatter of doubt?

So, that's part of my Noah and the Ark moment. Now, when I stare out my window, from my home by the water, and see the guys cleaning the yachts, I wonder, *Who built those?* I thought about all the physical labor that's behind great and small things, people we don't know or see. We can experience the miraculous by being responsible for the small and large tasks.

Be faithful to calling your dreams into being.

My desire is to always be a good steward of the responsibilities given to me. There's a ship builder's name that might be painted on the side that gets the credit, but it was actually several people who worked on different parts of these yachts. I won't see their names on the side. Although they may not be credited for their role in creating something of value, they finished the task for which they were responsible. Their contribution is evident. My calling is to be faithful and obedient to what the Lord has spoken and shown me to do.

His grace has always shown up in various ways and proven to

be sufficient for that part of the task. Until it's done!

I encourage you to rethink and explore your own spiritual experiences. Ask the questions of God that are most important to you and be prepared to listen. He will answer. He will speak. Whatever your version of a ship may be, build it as your passion project. Put your heart into it.

It's my hope and prayer that you will be drawn into a new experience so meaningful and joyful that others are at a lost for understanding. Know that you are a source of encouragement to many. I believe the world is anxious to have you bring your best self forward.

Got to Give It Up

MARVIN GAYE

REMOTE CONTROLS

"Unfortunately, real life doesn't have a remote control."

SIMONE ELKELES

Who's really in control? Often, I like to think that I am, but it doesn't always work the way I anticipate.

Recently, I was the emcee at our church family retreat. Before I stepped on stage as emcee at our church function, we sang "10,000 Reasons (Bless the Lord)." The song caught my heart and, quite unexpectedly, I was in tears as I approached the mic. When I reached it, I paused, unapologetically searching for answers to the emotions streaming forth. Apparently, I was quiet just the right amount of time for the audience to also ponder the words that had just come from their mouths. I found my words and shared them, and I'd like to share them with you.

We have two large screen, high-definition televisions in our home. They're both the same model, and the remotes are interchangeable. On any given evening, except during March Madness and NBA playoffs, my husband tends to spend time watching a show with me. Now, we have different TV viewing styles and the same is true for how we read books. He keeps his reading materials in the restroom, on his desk, and as audiobooks in his car. I keep mine on the nightstand, on the fireplace hearth, near the sofa, on the dining room table, on bookshelves, and as audiobooks in my car. We seldom read the same type of books but sharing a movie is possible. Because he works late and I tend to rise early, we have to find a middle-ground time to connect. This is how the conversation sometimes unfolds when he phones me from his car to say he's on his way home—my cue to try and stay awake.

"Are we going to watch the next episode of *Queen Sugar?*" he'll ask with sincere anticipation.

"Oh, sure," I say. "I already watched it, but that's not a problem."

"We left off at episode three last night," he says. "Are you on four and I can just catch up?"

"Sure."

Noticing I didn't answer what episode I'm on he asks, "How far ahead of me *are* you?"

"I finished it," I shamelessly answer.

"You finished the whole season, Babe, and you weren't even home until an hour ago?" He knows me so well.

"Yes," I say matter-of-factly. "I needed to see where it was going and if it was worth the time and energy to go through every episode. It is, so I skipped around in the other episodes for the gist of the story. So now we can pick up where we left off." Obviously, I can't see him because I'm on the sofa at home and he's on an LA freeway. But I know him so well too. I'm certain he's shaking his head. When he gets home, I don't tell him the ending and we pick up where we left off—episode three. I just have a little more knowledge of the show than he does, but he doesn't ask for what I know, and I've learned not to offer.

Another common scenario that didn't last long was when we'd start a show together and I'd want to skip ahead, so I'd take the remote control and fast forward. Unexpectedly, the image on the screen would stop and rewind. I'd look at my remote control, puzzled, try again, but again the image on the screen would stop, pause, and rewind. Before I learned the truth about what was going on (my husband was secretly holding the other remote), I'd get up and ask him to wait while I rummaged through drawers for the right size batteries. "No need to look," he'd say. "I've got it covered." It took a few of these episodes of dueling remote controls before I realized what was really going on. We had to decide who was actually going to be in control. Me, with my perfectly rational viewing style, or him, with his equally perfectly rational patient viewing style? We couldn't have two people running things, pretending that both of us could be in control.

Who's in control varies now. Sometimes, he acquiesces to me and says, "Okay, let me know when you've decided what we're going to watch *together*, and I'll come back when *you're* ready." So I do. Other times, he looks at me, we burst out laughing and say, "Who's in control of the remote controls tonight?" If I'm half asleep anyway, it's him. If I'm almost wide awake, I'll pause, smile, and because the most valued opportunity in the moment is that he made it home safely, we're together, and whatever makes him smile and want to be near me is a good place for me to lead from a place of joy, and because he feels the same about me, we find a way for one of us to let go of our attempt to have the remote control.

The words to "10,000 Reasons (Bless the Lord)" reminded me of God's patience. Often, in life, I want to skip ahead and find out where all of the life stuff is going down and if I can just get a glimpse into how the various stories of my life end? Do I succeed? Do I heal? How does a particular prayer get answered? These and so much more are examples of why I want to rush ahead. My point of view seems quite rational. If I could just rush away and find out if I'm successful on a particular project, or if the real estate deal is going to close and the money will land in our bank account, or if my long-awaited answered prayers for healing, recovery, and whatever my desired outcomes are will really happen, then I'd feel better and be more patient about the time and energy required to go through it all. The song reminded me that because of my faith, I've already been given a glimpse into the end, and it's all good. It's all very good, and I trust that the processes of daily life work together for good.

The song reminded me to be patient when parts of life's journey are slow, awkward, difficult to understand, and sometimes just too hard to watch. The same is true when I can't control my hopes for others; I'm reminded of my own insufficiencies and flaws. I need to be patient. I have no more control over when the phone will ring and I hear my son's voice saying, "Happy Mother's Day" or "Happy Father's Day" than I can control whether friends with young children will be open to my well-intended suggestions to have their children explore new foods and cultures with others I introduce them to. I'm simply reminded that all I'm in control of is making sure that I, for example, pick up the phone earlier in the day to express the same good wishes of love to others that I am desiring to receive.

I have a friend who worked herself into an absolute tizzy fit because her son had purchased a large screen TV for his dorm room his freshman year of college. He was attending school two states over, more than an eight-hour drive and two-hour plane ride away. I watched as my friend, phone to her ear, paced her kitchen floor, yelling at her son about being irresponsible, and how a new TV wasn't going to help him with success in his college classes. Her demands for him to return it echoed throughout her empty nest.

In frustration and disbelief, she hung up the phone and proceeded to try and pull words of agreement out of me. I guess I was silent for too long. She stopped and said adamantly, "You tell him! He will listen to you! I'm going to call him back. You tell him, Gael-Sylvia, that you agree and if he wants to be in control of his life that he needs to be more responsible!"

I've had to remind myself many times during the subsequent years of the words I spoke to her: "Girl, how in the world are you going to be in control this far away? How does being so remote allow any of us to control what he does? From way over here, none of us can control (I wanted to say 'no one *should* control') when he sleeps, when he studies, and when he turns that television on or off, or when and if he returns it. You've done the best you could to raise him to be responsible. Maybe now's a good time to release control. All of us love him, but let's be real, none of us has remote control. He's a growing man. Trust that he'll do the right thing and be alright."

To give is a way of releasing my remote control, my need to control, or to at least feel that I have some control. Singing this song and remembering those words to my friend and myself were the raw reminders and enough to make me pause and bring this girl to tears. The song reminded me that the view may not be the same from where I am and where God is. I can't pretend that I'm in control of everything. So I choose to release my inclination to have remote control. I let go and let God. When I'm tired, it's easier to roll over and say, "Have it your way." When I'm more awake and energetic, and my eyes feel wide open to all the possibilities I can make happen, that's when I try to set the pace for when and how things will get done. When I'm in control and can do things my way, I can manage my time, my To-Do List, and perhaps the outcomes. If I want to do life alone, that may work, but when doing it together with others and God, the response is often the same: "Let me know when you've decided what we're going to watch *together*, and I'll come back when you're ready." And I do.

I encourage you to try and release something today that you're trying to control. Perhaps it's a circumstance or relationship where you make six steps forward quickly and then seven steps back, having to not only start over again as you ponder what happened, but step back even farther because you didn't get the outcome you were anticipating when you rushed ahead justifying your rational approach. What may always seem rational to you may not be the only perspective and approach to enjoying life, especially when you want to experience it with heart and eyes wide open. Release. Look for the most valued opportunity in the moment and lead with that from a place of joy.

It's my hope and prayer that you be surrounded by moments of peace, joy, and laughter whether you're in direct control, alone, or with others. May you seize every opportunity to value the moment. Be patient with yourself. Speak kindly to yourself and others. We don't have to be in control of everything, and all of life isn't always serious. Laugh out loud and frequently. And may every dramatic episode, within every chapter of your life, be led by joy.

May you personally experience the joy and the freedom of releasing control and not always having a need to rush ahead to try and figure out the endings.

You Know My Name
TASHA COBBS

CHOOSE JOY

*"Keep your eyes focused on what is right,
and look straight ahead to what is good."*

PROVERBS 4:25

"They say a person needs just three things to be truly happy in this world: someone to love, something to do, and something to hope for." Lying in my bed, pondering this line from author Tom Bodett, I thought, *I have someone to love. In fact, I have lots of someones to love.* Yet I wanted to add more—more people to love, more hope, more possibilities of greater purpose—by making sure that my broken heart healed, all parts open to flow freely with love.

I then thought of the e.e. cummings line, "The most wasted of all days is one without laughter." I chose not to let another day be wasted. I would regain hope. I would laugh again. I would play. The first game of play would be solitary; that's what the emotional and physical isolation during that time dictated. I would savor my time of solitude and play a game of Hide and Seek looking to recover joy and laughter. I don't recall the exact moment I made this resolution during that tough time of recovery. Most likely, it was a series of moments stacked one upon another over the years like a child's building blocks with alphabet letters and images on each side. Some fell, yet others were of a sure foundation, not budging from their role, waiting to be reengaged in play. A child plays effortlessly, instinctively. But as an adult, I had to be intentional in learning to play and relearning life skills through the art of play. Life had offered me the opportunity to accept the gift of a new set of building blocks within my toy chest of older versions.

A child learns science when their construction blocks fall and they observe gravity. Through building, they learn the use of simple machines such as ramps. They learn new words and language skills as they explore each new game and toy. This falling and learning and bouncing back is all part of their play. And play fills them with joy. I would have to shift my thinking to see where I could find joy in the fall. I, too, would need to ramp up my intake of play, learn new language skills and vocabulary as I talked to myself about what was being created anew.

I decided to no longer be defined solely by what I did (or had done), what I owned (or had owned), whom I knew, and what I'd accomplished. Although those things remained true to a part of who I am, I didn't want the language or emphasis on the past. Nor did I want to see that happen in the future. I wanted the character and heart of who I truly am to be the foundation on which I would rebuild my life. And I would have fun doing it.

Building blocks are particularly beneficial for children between the ages of eighteen months to three years old because they help younger children master motor skills. My adult building blocks had no age limit. While children learn consequences, gravity, and spatial skills from building blocks, playing with my adult blocks would help me develop new cognitive skills, especially problem-solving skills, to navigate the uncharted territory I found myself in. I'd also build the big-girl skills I so needed. Peace. Joy. Laughter.

FIRST STEP. I would be still. Be quiet. Be intentional in nourishing myself to health with megavitamins of faith and hope for the cellular building blocks of my soul. I'd keep it simple and start right then and there from where I lay. No need to wait and see what would happen before choosing to start. There was no need to wait for divine intervention, a bolt of lightning, a surprise phone call, an unexpected check—those things did happen, but only after I had decided to "get on up" in my decision to be joyful again. Life had already happened and there was no reason not to start anew within that very moment.

SECOND STEP. I vowed to continue my morning routine of a Gratitude Walk. You're probably wondering how I planned to continue a Gratitude Walk if I was pretty much bedridden. As Minnie Ripperton sang, I would "take a little trip through my mind and explore it." If beauty is in the eye of the beholder, then I could not merely look at the world around me, going through it too fast and too self-preoccupied, with beautiful details whizzing past unnoticed. I needed to see, really see it. So I would take gratitude walks through my mind, searching for the details, for good in as many things as possible, and acknowledge them instead of simply walking by. I would acknowledge what was beautiful, pure, whatever was lovely, whatever I could find admirable, excellent and in so doing say, "Thank you, Lord. Thank you." Then, when I was stronger, I'd resume my actual walks, building strength and adding distance each day. And after that, I'd add an evening walk.

THIRD STEP. I'd continue to spend Quiet Time Devotionals with my Bible, colored pens by my side and journal wide open. That's why I've included illustrations in this book, for you to experience the peace and pleasure of child-like coloring. Color! Try it! Make it bright! Make it fun! Make it bold! Make it you! And write. Write. Write. Writing allows your soul to have a chance to speak. Writing records what your eyes have seen and your lips can't speak. Quiet Time with my God helps me hear what I otherwise would have unintentionally shut out and to recapture what would have slipped away.

FOURTH STEP: Continue my Song of the Day, which recalibrates my emotions and redirects my mind when it tries to wander toward negative or discouraging thoughts. This practice helps me learn to listen with fresh ears to the sounds that exist even when there is silence — the sound of my own thoughts and feelings, the sound of instruments that I may have missed before.

FIFTH STEP. I'd stick to my practice of selecting a Picture of the Day—a mental picture I'd bring forward—to keep my mind fine-tuned to actively look for the good in the details around me. I saw (and still see) that beauty in the details as God saying He's still here with me. My mind and soul were starving for creative nourishment, not the kind that comes from intellectually processing information. I needed a balance between having no words to say (I had no words for all that was happening. I was in a perpetual loss for words.) and lots of pictures speaking a thousand words on my behalf. I was too weak and exhausted to actively grasp for more intellectual stimulation, but I did have a thirst for more knowledge through images feeding the whole of me holistically through impressions, intuitions, and feelings. "The act of looking brings me into focus" is as true for me as it is for Julia Cameron.

And so I started. One morning, during my Quiet Time Devotional, while reading Samuel 1 and 2 in the Holy Bible, I noticed that many paragraphs opened with the words, "In the course of time." In that moment, I was reminded that recovery takes time. There would be no quick fixes, but I could take quick steps to start the journey. I had to be more intentional in preserving my energy. I could no longer justify the sacrifice of brain cells, unproductive conversations with people who would drain me, or circumstances that would cause me to waste a single day without the presence of peace, joy, and laughter.

While these practices had, in some form, been a part of my daily routine, they took on new meaning. I began to go deeper. I stopped asking, *What else could happen? What else could go terribly wrong?* for fear life would reveal there was still more. Instead, I asked, *What else could be brighter and more appreciated while it's still right in front of me?* I searched. I meant to find each brighter detail and thought and hold onto it, for the singular purpose of being able to release it again. My hope was that I could release it into the life of others as a reminder that there is still an abundance of good around us and that there is, indeed, a good, good Father, Creator of All.

In the course of time, I found myself waking with an urge to enjoy the new day, to have adventures of faith seeking new life experiences hidden within each day. In the loneliest of moments, I would invite the companionship of joy and laughter to fill my day. I listened. I would find ways to make a way for myself, inside myself, and find a new way of looking—not back at how things used to be (and were no longer) but forward.

Over time, I found my words changing. Joy came out of me during playful experiences and in serious moments. Laughter reminded me that not everything is to be taken seriously. Joy had become my barometer, laughter my thermostat, and peace my insurance for my well-being. In new ways, I feel covered in all circumstances.

I encourage you to focus on joy. Think about who and what can help you add joy to your day. Be more intentional in preserving your energy and choose one playful experience to engage in this week. Smile. Let there be one intentional reason to laugh. Pick something that brings you joy: Wear your favorite outfit (never underestimate the power of a good outfit on a bad day!). Go to the park and sit in a swing (you'll surprise yourself when your legs naturally start pumping, sending you back to a happy childhood memory). Go outside, stare at city lights at night from a high place. Anything that makes you smile. Keep it simple. Enjoy the moment and just let it be. Eliminate excess of anything or anything that isn't needed. Release the people who bring you down; exchange their toxicity with joy. Choose to make one small change in your habits. Perhaps step away for a few hours from that one person who brings you down and add one person who inspires you and lifts your spirit up. Watch the direction of your life change exponentially as you live by choosing joy as your barometer.

It's my hope and prayer for you that you'll choose not to waste another precious moment without the presence of peace, joy, and laughter.

ACKNOWLEDGEMENTS

I am in awe. Overcome with joy and gratitude that my small dream of more than forty years would be remembered by such a big God. I am humbly thankful for the reminder that all of us are important to The One who created us, and no matter how long it may seem to take for our dreams to be fulfilled or our prayers answered, nothing is being ignored. Day by day, I've been learning how to stop expecting the worst and, instead, look for the good around me, how to truly experience that "the joy of the LORD is my strength." (Nehemiah 8:10)

I want to take this opportunity to acknowledge those who have been a special part of my life journey and to say Thank you. The list is long and a reflection of how blessed I am, so please, please forgive me if I momentarily forget to add your name on this page after forty years on this journey. Rest assured, I know who you are, and I hope you also know that you are truly special to me and that your presence is reflected within the stories of this book.

To Lisa Tener, a new lifelong friend and book coach. You restored my confidence and surrounded me with flowers, wisdom, and others who could hear what I wanted to say. I am truly appreciative of you. Thank you for the many introductions.

To Kelly Malone! WOW! Without your laughter, stories of your own crazy-cool grandmother, and your impeccable editing gifts, I don't know if I would have crossed the finish line as rapidly as we did. Thank you, too, to your husband, Tom Frankenberg. May more Jewish men be blessed by the stories he helped edit. Thank you, Tom!

To Melissa Davis. You didn't see this coming, did you? Keep writing those grants for Girls Fly! and helping me "get those girls."

To Tamara Monosoff, book coach and retreat roommate. May we have many more impromptu dances under the Mexican moonlight celebrating the joy of new friendships. Thank you for your referral to the amazing graphic designer, Erika Ruggiero, who designed the cover and interior of this book.

Thanks to Mary Lane Potter for your spot-on proofreading.

Hi, Dad and Mom, Sorrell and Audrey Brown. You danced with us, baked with us, and affirmed the power of our faith in Christ, and taught us the ways to love and to fight for the good of others. To my siblings, Allen, Barbara, and Joice, and in memory of Bill. Reverend Jarnagin, may this chapter be among your most joyful ever!

In memory of Beatrice Odessa Ritchie, my paternal grandmother, who went from being a sharecropper to a housekeeper to a philanthropist. You believed in me and responded with every sweet potato pie you sold in front of the grocery stores and at Friendship Baptist Church to make sure I went to Switzerland.

To my wonderful in-laws and cheerleaders, John and Frances Pullen, and to Aunt Sis, Mary Tyson, and my cousins, nieces, and nephews. Dayna, Isabella, Elijah and Jeremiah; Cheryl, Courtni and Desiree; A.J., Misti, Marquex, Michael, Lois, Ben, Richard, Marcus, and all of your children, may you see your names in books that you write, and may this be a reminder of how much you are loved.

To the children God sent, who allow Mark and me to have godchildren: Garett, Sabrina, and Josh Yee; Asenth Murphy and her amazing husband, Steven; Jeff and Jenn Nakao and Jessica (Nakao) and Joey Stallmeyer—and all your children; and Evelyn Luna Ramirez and her children Gianna, Isaiah, and Carrie Dam.

To our Seed's and Evergreen church family! You are the story within the stories and the dream come true. We are forever thankful and blessed because of your love. A special thank you to Pastor Kyle and Carol Shimazaki and your four loving children: Trent, Faith, Caleb, and Selah. You make tremendous sacrifices and each and every one is appreciated.

To the parents and children of all the birthday and graduation celebrations I missed because of this book, may this be an eternal gift and make up for my absence: Susan, Scott, Morgan, and Ian Rhodewalt; Marina and Marten Forskosh, Greyden and Graham Chin, Maddox Kiyohara, the Diodati Family of Melissa, Miriam, Mercie, Melanie, Moses; Nathan, Lyane, Hallie, Gabbie, Emi, and Shane Peralta; Nora Lui, Grace Yoshimoto, and Janita Gordon; Walter and Jaron Lee; Gloria and Randy Furukawa; Ada Yeh; Fred Kawashima; the Demas family; David Johns; and the one who always went the extra mile, Cathleen "Cat" Miles.

ABOUT THE AUTHOR

Gael-Sylvia works globally with industry and community leaders to uncover the good around them. Doing so positively affects the behavior and decision-making abilities needed to recover from loss, increase leadership development, and create a productive, balanced life by leading from a place of joy.

A former co-owner in the largest minority-owned commercial real estate brokerage firm in the state of California, Gael-Sylvia is the CEO of Girls Fly!, a transformational leadership company dedicated to developing high-functioning teams, and a retired award-winning McDonald's franchisee.

Her path to approval as a hotel franchisee, ownership of a bilingual business radio broadcast, studies at the prestigious Waseda University in Tokyo, time served in the Peace Corp, and years in government relations positioned her for economic and philanthropic growth. Then the Great Recession hit, multiple deaths occurred, and a debilitating health condition kept Gael-Sylvia bedridden for fifteen months. During that time, she launched Sylvia Global Media Network, a global empowerment program, discovered the good around her, and after research and experimentation, developed a program designed to help herself and others live and lead from a place of joy.

Gael-Sylvia has recovered from her illness and returned to being a joyful, healthy wife, mother, grandmother, ballroom dancer, and advocate for all who believe in happy endings. She lives in Seal Beach, California, with her husband of forty plus happy years.

The Good around Us: Living and Leading from a Place of Joy, Even in the Joyless Moments is the first in a series of books Gael-Sylvia is writing about business, personal growth, and leadership. The series focuses on personal growth, philanthropy, and business, including empowering employees and community engagement to go beyond brand, goodwill, and profitability.

She would love to hear from you. You can contact her at Gaelsylviapullen.com.

Made in the USA
San Bernardino, CA
21 May 2020